2,000 MILES AROUND THE TREE OF LIFE

A NATURALIST HIKES THE APPALACHIAN TRAIL

A PEACE CORPS WRITERS BOOK

RICHARD W. CARROLL

2,000 Miles Around the Tree of Life:
A Naturalist Hikes the Appalachian Trail
A Peace Corps Writers Book
An imprint of Peace Corps Worldwide

ISBN-10: 1935925512
ISBN-13: 9781935925514

First Peace Corps Writers Edition, November, 2014

This walk and these words are dedicated to my mother,
Lillian Mae Wolcott Carroll, Lill the Flower Lady,
who made the love of nature a natural part of my life.

Love
 is the nectar that
 flows through the
 Tree of Life,
Giving beauty to the
 flowers, form to the
 fruit,
Vibrating like a harp string
 between heaven and earth,
 strummed by the seasons tuned
 by the sun.

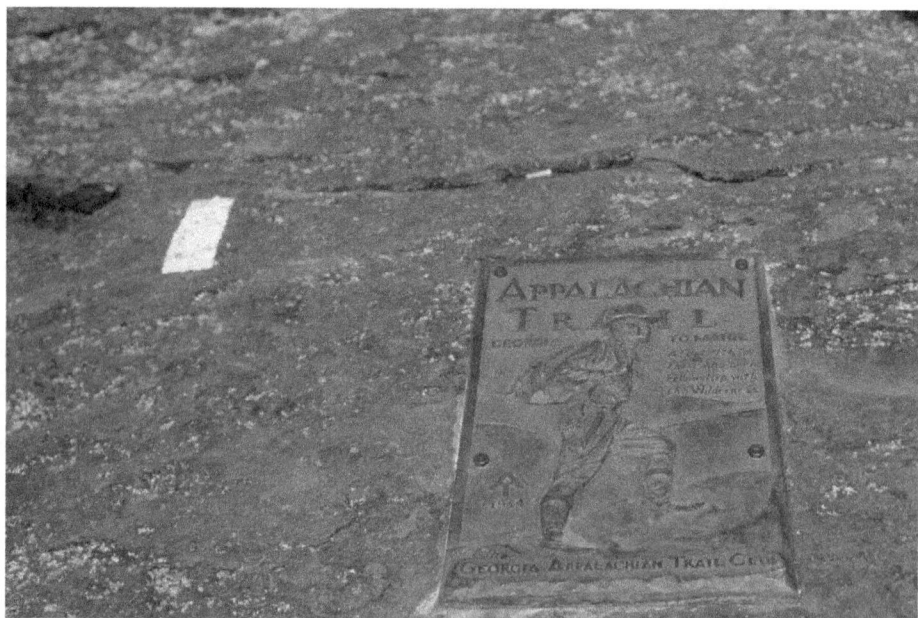

Plaque on Springer Mountain.

PREFACE

I walked the Appalachian Trail in 1975, in a journey that spanned five months and one day. I stepped across the engraved plaque marking the southern terminus of the A.T., set in the stone of Springer Mountain, Georgia, on April 14, and climbed Mt. Katahdin, Maine, via the Knife Edge Trail, on September 15. The northern terminus was dusted with snow. I would have completed this climb the day before, but it had snowed on the mountain, and the park service closed the trail. So I wound up experiencing all four seasons on the Appalachian Trail. I rested in a shelter, let my guard down, and got a commemorative hole in my pack from a mouse rummaging around for the remnants of the food I carried. After five months of hanging my pack, boots, food bag, and anything edible or sweaty in trees, to stave off bears, porcupines, and other woodland residents, on the last day I shared a meal with a mouse. I later sewed my A.T. Thru-Hiker patch over the hole, honoring this breach.

I had started the A.T. in May of 1974, beginning at Mt. Katahdin and heading south. I went with two friends from my hometown of Cheshire, Connecticut. It was a beautiful beginning, with glorious views from the summit. As we reached the famous Hundred-Mile Wilderness, the confluence of warming air and a trail that was soggy from the spring snowmelt sent clouds of blackflies into the air and heading straight for our bodies. Citronella and head nets didn't quite keep them at bay, and nothing is as annoying as black-flies under your head net. One friend had insulated boots, which were none-theless saturated by the dampness of the swampy woods, and his feet were peeling away. The other had a severe reaction to the blackfly bites. We came across a skidder on a logging road, I started it up and drove us out to a main road, and we hitchhiked out of there. I then joined my sister, Lynn, on a four-month tour of the national parks of the Western United States, and began the A.T. again the next spring, this time alone.

I was brought up on a small farm in Cheshire, with as many as ten thou-sand turkeys free-ranging in the back lot. It was rather intimidating for a young boy to look eye-to-wattle with those turkeys as I made my way to my cousin's house next door. My mother was known as Lill the Flower Lady. She was considered the naturalist-in-residence, and I was Mother Nature's son. Anyone who found a snake or a turtle would bring it to her to identify. She ran a nature center at Camp Laurel Hill, a Girl Scout camp in our town. She taught principles of conservation biology to my sister and me as kids, and we were instilled with a love and respect for nature. This was the foundation that would support me throughout my career, and in every aspect of my life.

Cheshire was a farm town then, mostly dairy. Now most of those farms grow McMansions. This transition was just beginning during my hike in 1975. I kept a journal along the way, and the local newspaper, the *Cheshire Herald*, published a series of articles based on those entries, which have been adapted for this book. I was committed to instilling a sense of pride in our agricultural and natural history. The developers ultimately won out. I go back maybe once every five years and drive through subdivisions and remember where we rode horses, played in the woods, and worked on farms. A paradigm shift has taken place, and most of the current residents are completely unaware of what the town once was. Life moves on.

I used to sit with my grandmother when I was in high school. She was in her nineties, and I would ask her what life was like when she was a girl. She reminisced about horse races on Whaley Avenue, in New Haven, and a relative's blacksmith shop that stood where a highway connector is now. Our collective memory is shallow. We have little knowledge of the past, except for a few stories from perhaps the two generations of family and friends we may have known.

My five months on the A.T. in 1975 were pivotal for me. I had just graduated from Southern Connecticut State College, in New Haven, in the spring of 1974 with a B.S. in marine biology. What does one do with a B.S. in marine biology? Thousands of recent graduates across the country were asking themselves the same question. My marine biology professor suggested that I apply to the Peace Corps to get real-life experience in the field. I applied. My parents met me in the Shenandoahs and brought an invitation to go to the Philippines to raise shrimp. Besides the fact that I was now about halfway finished with the trail, and had no inclination to hang up my boots, I did not want to be a G.I. Joe under the dictatorship of Ferdinand Marcos, so I turned down the offer.

I thought that would be the last that I would hear from the Peace Corps. When I finished the two thousand miles and hitchhiked home, another invitation urged me to go to the Central African Republic to raise fish. In 1976, I left for C.A.R., as far from the mountains and ocean as one can get on this earth. I was a Peace Corps Volunteer there for five years, first working as a fisheries extension agent in villages and then as a wildlife biologist studying black rhino and elephants. Later I did research for a dissertation on gorilla feeding ecology for a PhD from the Yale School of Forestry and

Environmental Studies. This led to a 35-year career at the World Wildlife Fund heading the Africa and Madagascar Programs. But that's another few books away—stay tuned!

Truly, the A.T. was a turning point in my life. It was the first significant thing I set out to do and finished. The satisfaction of doing something so grand was a revelation—to have experienced every moment from beginning to end. As I look back 40 years later, I can see that this trail guided me toward my path as a biologist dedicated to keeping life alive on this earth. It has been "right livelihood" done personally, physically, and from the heart. The Appalachian Trail was marked with white blazes, which led to other journeys marked by intuition and inspiration. I have had a good life, with three great children walking their own paths. All I tell them is to follow their hearts.

The author on Katahdin Peak, the northern terminus of the A.T.

ONE

Where do I begin to tell the story of my hike on the Appalachian Trail? Do I start with Springer Mountain, the actual southern terminus of the trail? Or do I begin with the 6.9-mile approach trail from Amicalola Falls State Park, in Dawson County, Georgia, with its spectacular five-hundred-foot waterfall?

I think I should go back even further, to the hours of daydreaming that came well before the planning and long before the reality of two thousand miles of wilderness hiking.

I read somewhere that if an idea is still alive and strong in your mind after at least a year of planning—a year of of setbacks, of considering alternatives, of exploring opportunities—it must be something you really want to do. So the first challenge of the Appalachian Trail was not physical but rather a challenge of my will to even begin such a journey.

Next came the planning of the route. I had to know where I was going so I could get there! That meant buying the guidebooks to the Appalachian Trail. There were eleven of these, each describing in detail a section of the trail. This set cost about fifty dollars. In addition, I had the Appalachian Trail Mileage Fact Sheet, which provides a handy reference to the distances between shelters and landmarks. This was one dollar and fifty cents.

Now that I knew where I was going, I needed the equipment to get me there. Just the right pack: a Kelty Tioga, which I slightly modified with the addition of two new pockets for greater accessibility to my gear. I chose Kelty because of its reputation for strength and endurance, the convenience and comfort. The next thing to consider was a sleeping bag. It had to be light and warm, so naturally I chose a Sierra Design goose-down bag. This high quality frame pack cost about fifty-five dollars, while the sleeping bag was eighty-four dollars. This seems like a lot of money, but it's brought me a lifetime of camping equipment. And, of course, of utmost importance are the boots. Mine were made by Rieker and are fairly stiff, well padded, with Vibram soles.

The rest of my equipment includes a poncho, rain chaps, pack rain cover, tube tent for emergency shelter, space blanket for ground cloth, foam pad, Gerry mini-stove with fuel bottles, first aid kit, quart canteen, new rope, toilet paper, three pairs of ragg socks, two pairs of inner socks, a pair of sneakers, a pair of pants, two towels, washcloth, flashlight, knife, camera with wrist harness, film, pen and writing pad, as well as food. I packaged up staples such as granola, powdered milk, oatmeal for colder times, raisins, rice cakes, peanut butter, honey, fratina—a soy and vegetable protein mixture, soup, and Durkee instant omelets. I arranged to have care packages sent to post offices in towns near the trail. Occasional treats from home as well as occasional goodies growing along the trail will spice up my menu.

I had to arrange to get from Cheshire, Connecticut, to Amicalola Falls State Park, in Georgia. I called the WPLR Ride Board and got a ride with a young couple named Jim and Mary to Route 26 in South Carolina. Then I was on my own, hitching through the notorious redneck-filled South.

After a series of very rapid, very pleasant rides with some of the friendliest people I've ever met, I found myself in the Cumming, Georgia, general store, around 6:00 P.M. on a Saturday, about thirty miles from Amicalola Falls State Park, where the trail begins.

That's where I met Charles Goff in his Ford Falcon. He and his side-kick, Jim Coffin, gave me a ride, a box of Kentucky Fried Chicken, and a complete history and tour of Dawson County, Georgia. It started with a ride past a house that belongs to Junior from the "Hee Haw" show, then past a number of mountaineers' shacks, past the only moonshine museum in the country and right to my campsite in Amicalola Falls.

Bidding them goodbye at sunset, I found myself in the midst of a church group around a campfire, being fed s'mores and answering all kinds of personal questions. Everyone was friendly and interested. Finally I laid out my space blanket, foam pad, and sleeping bag, climbed in and watched the stars and listened to my first night in the woods.

The next morning I awoke with frost on my sleeping bag and a chill in my bones. I fired up my stove, had some oatmeal and an orange from the charitable church people, and was off on the approach trail leading to the beginning of the Appalachian Trail. Most of this mountainous area, which extends north to the North Carolina border, is in the Chattahoochee National Forest. The approach trail on this clear, cool day brought me through woods predominantly of white oak. Black oak, chestnut oak, tulip, and dogwood were also common. If it weren't for the holly trees and the mistletoe, which is parasitic in the oaks here, these woods would be similar to my own.

I guess it's a fair exchange—we get the snow in our yards for Christmas; they, hardy mistletoe in theirs. The dogwood, which was in bloom in the lower areas and Atlanta, was only in the bud stage at this elevation. Spring hasn't yet reached the mountains, so I'm getting the benefit of watching things come alive. So up over Frost Mountain, at 3,400 feet, and the 6.9

miles to Springer Mountain. On the Appalachian Trail I signed my name in the register and started following the white blazes. Springer forms the apex of a great "V" formed by the splitting of the Blue Ridge chain in Virginia.

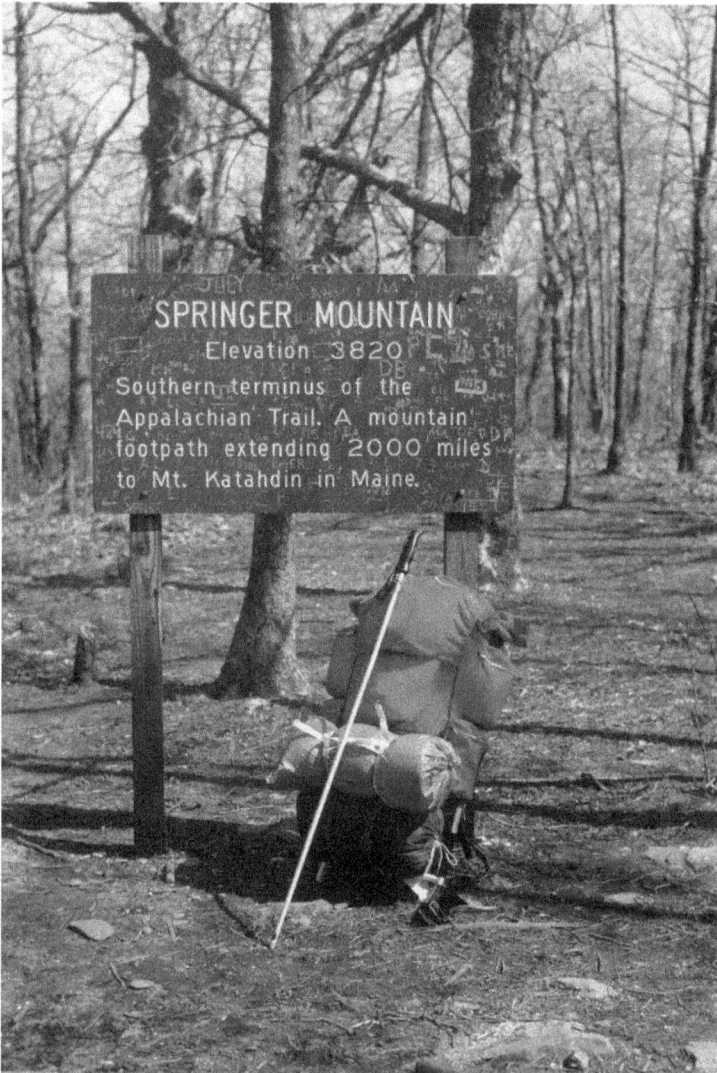

Springer Mountain, southern terminus of the A.T.

Follow the white blazes.

The bloodroot in full smiling bloom along the trail seemed to be applauding me with their leaves as if I were a Fourth of July parade with my massive float on my back. I heard the junglelike calls and the jackhammerings of a pileated woodpecker, and the calls of the mocking-bird—the master mimic—and the magical, fluid songs of warblers were everywhere. My old friend the tiger swallowtail fluttered around me welcoming me to his domain.

Clouds were building up rapidly. I decided to spend my first night in Big Stamp lean-to. I went down to the spring for water, and fired up my stove. I added two cups of boiling water to a mass of orange cubes and watched them turn into carrots before my very eyes. A little space-age wonder in my primitive life. After I ate, I gathered up a few sticks for a fire so that on this dark and starless night I'd have the warm company of glowing tinders to lull me into a trance.

As the fire died, so did my energy, so I climbed into my sleeping bag all set for a good night's sleep, but I wasn't alone. Little feet running nervously back and forth startled me awake. Did you ever try to fight your way out of a mummy bag in a hurry? I got a lot of practice that night. I figured out that it was time to transfer my food from my pack into a stuff bag and hang it from a nail on the roof rafter. Back to sleep, right? Wrong. Just as I was dozing off I again heard feet—larger ones outside the lean-to. After another fight out of my mummy bag, I found my flashlight, grabbed my walking stick, and, shaking nervously, listened as the night stalker rounded the front of the lean-to. On went the flashlight—down crashed the stick, and there stood a completely indifferent skunk. Fortunately, he didn't raise a stink about it and went about his business, so I tried to ignore him. I made it through the night.

I awoke to a rainy, foggy dawn. I had my breakfast, donned my pack, and was off through the jungles of rhododendron. The thick fog, dense vegetation, and the call of the pileated woodpecker made it seem like a tropical rain forest.

Went about nine miles to Hawk Mountain lean-to, got out of my wet clothes and into my sleeping bag, and had some hot tea. Then along came Mike from Pennsylvania. I hung my poncho and space blanket over the front of the shelter to keep out the wind and rain.

The next day was still cloudy and windy. Went twenty miles to Blood Mountain, which is the highest point on the trail in Georgia. The shelter was made of stone and was like a barn. Of course, the usual mice and skunk were visitors at night.

Awoke the next morning with the sun shining through the cracks in the wooden windows of the shelter. It was the perfect blend of sun and wind to make hiking in shorts comfortable. I hung all my damp clothes from the day before on my pack. I stopped at Neel's Gap, took a bath in the men's room sink, and stocked up on freeze-dried food. Moved on and saw a lot of towhees and juncos in the bushes and hawks circling overhead. About five miles ahead at Tesnatee Gap, I met Mary Jo, a 67-year-old hiker, going to Damascus, Tennessee, about 450 miles ahead. We soaked our feet together in an ice-cold stream, then I moved on.

I got to Low Gap shelter at about 6:30. It was like the Hilton—it even had an outhouse! I took a bath in one of the creeks, had supper, then enjoyed the sunset and watched the stars rise.

The next day I went from Low Gap to Tray Mountain, about fifteen miles. The first part was like skipping down Lullaby Lane. As the day went on, the trail got tougher with a lot of steep ups and downs. At Tray Mountain lean-to, I met a group of boys from a special school. They treated me to dinner, and we all squeezed into the shelter.

Woke the next morning to the sunrise and the singing of birds and was serenaded by them all day. At about 9 A.M. I found a coot sleeping under a log with his head tucked under his wing. I took his picture and moved on. Met my friend Mike again at Plum Orchard Gap, and we hiked on together. We went a few more miles, found a nice spot in the woods near a spring, and had a good supper of pea soup, carrots, potatoes, onions, and chocolate pudding. I had to set up my tube tent, as it began to sprinkle in the middle of the night.

Trailing arbutus.

Woke up to another cloudy day, but the birds still sang. Mike and I hiked together and reached the Georgia-North Carolina border at Bly Gap at about 9 A.M. We met a lot of weekend groups in spite of the weather. Normally, I see very few other people hiking. Had to break out the poncho again and went over Standing Indian Ridge through the groves of laurel and rhododendron to Carter Gap shelter, about fifteen miles. The shelter was full, so I set up my tube tent again. I'm just as happy staying away from the mouse-infested shelters anyway.

Sunday was a perfectly mellow day. Bloodroot in full array, trailing arbutus shyly showing its tiny bell-shaped flowers beneath the dry leaves at the trail's edge. Blue, yellow, and white violets, tiny bluets, the smell of pine, and the warmth of the sun. Climbed Mt. Andrews, 5,240 feet, with magnificent views. Walking along, I heard the drumming of a grouse, and once in a while one would fly up and startle me out of a trance. Camped near a brook under a clear sky with a half moon and the sound of an owl nearby.

Monday. I've gone about nineteen miles through the most spectacular scenery yet. The mountains are getting higher, and so am I. Spring is reaching the mountains, and everything is coming to life. The sun dances down through the pale young leaves as they burst from the buds that enclosed them for so long.

Crossed Siler Bald and Wayah Bald, 5,336 feet with views of Mt. Mitchell, which is the highest mountain east of the Rockies. Stopped a few miles ahead to soak my aching feet in one of those cool, clear springs and washed out some clothes. I looked like a walking laundry rack. Spent the night in an abandoned fire tower on Wesser Bald with fantastic 360-degree views of nothing but mountains blanketed by a mystical haze and tinted by the sunset.

Packed the next morning as the sun was rising and moved on down toward the town of Wesser. Hiked down through Wesser Creek Valley. The lower slopes were covered with white trillium, anemone, violets, mayapple, and occasional dogwood. The trail came out on Wesser Creek Road, a dirt road through some real beautiful farms with front porches, rocking chairs, and smoke coming from the chimneys. The mountain came down to the back doors, and each had its garden spot, a few cows, chickens, goats, and a brook in the front. Walked into Wesser and got a room in the Nantahala Outdoor Center on the river. Got a real good meal that wasn't freeze-dried, a shower, and a good night's sleep before moving on to the most difficult part of the entire Appalachian Trail. This next section brought me out of the Nantahala National Forest and connects with the Smokies. Most of the trail in this twenty-five-mile stretch has been relocated. It goes straight up and straight down with no switchbacks, no breaks, and little water. It was one step at a time up "Jump Up," a climb straight up about 1,500 feet and up Cetoah Bald. The trail continued up and down. Going down is almost worse than going up. Your thighs and knees ache; your toes get squashed in the front of your boots. Hiked all day under oppressive heat and the threat of a thunderstorm. Had to stop due to rain and set up my tube tent. The next day I hiked fifteen miles to Fontana Village, where I was awaiting my camping pass into the Smokies.

So, for the last week and a half, I've walked through 160 miles of sheer awe-inspiring natural paradise. I've passed like a king through archways of rhododendron heralded by birdsong and mountain stream. I've passed over ridgetops and watched endless mountains roll like waves off into the sky. I've walked down slopes where the sun shone pale green through the young tree leaves onto a vast green carpeted forest floor studded with flowery gems. Whole hillsides of white trillium, white and pinkish anemone, white, blue, and yellow violets, buttercups and bluets, wild geranium and mayapple. And overhead, flowering dogwood and tulip trees. I've watched and listened for hours to the birds.

Rhododendron.

Though I am an alien in this timeless wilderness, I am thankful to my generous host who has unfolded its beauties before me. I feel it's a real honor to share a piece of this natural world with its inhabitants, and I walk softly through this delicate realm. It all leaves such a great impression on my mind—I feel it's my duty to leave as little an impression as possible on this earth. I just hope man in his impatience doesn't chop down this ancient tree of life, for whether he chooses to notice it or not, our little nest also lies within its branches.

This is the Southern Appalachian Trail, and I look ahead to 1,900 miles of wonderment.

TWO

After a night's layover in Fontana Village, a little tourist trap town about two miles from the trail, I managed to locate a ranger and get a camping permit for Great Smoky Mountains National Park. The ranger was real nice and gave me a ride from the village back to the trail. We sat talking in his truck until the rain slacked off, then I was on my way over the hill that came down to Fontana Dam, which is on the Little Tennessee River and is the southern boundary of the park. I crossed the dam and followed a gravel road around the algae-green lake to where the trail ascended into the Smokies. Here I shed my poncho despite the rain, since it was like a sauna in there and I was getting wetter inside than out.

Walking through these endless mountains, I got to thinking about spending five months as their guest, sharing this small parcel of time with the ageless wilderness. Five months, another growing season, another chance for the minute adaptations for life on an ever-changing planet. Five months compared to the eons of evolution behind each flower, each tree, and ourselves, one season of following a path deeper into a lifetime.

I hiked around a ridge, then up to a fire tower with incredible views, then on to Birch Spring lean-to, a day of only five miles but one full of many,

many, memories. There I met two ladies who were seeking the abundant warblers in the park. They taught me about the birds I'd been seeing and hearing. We saw hooded warblers, black and white warblers, blackburnian warblers, vireos and ovenbirds, phoebes and flycatchers. And yesterday a ruby-throated hummingbird nearly ran me down.

The shelters in the park are made of stone, with a fireplace, bunks, and a chain-link fence enclosure to keep out the bears. This morning, I noticed that the greens of the trees seemed to show more true, pure shades in cloudy, rainy times than when the sun bleaches the tones out of them.

A shelter in the Smokies.

Sunday morning, shorts and sunshine. Hiked through columns of yellow birch with snow flurries of spring beauties at their feet, with scattered adder's tongue looking like stars. Hiking along slowly and quietly, I saw two

14

white-tailed deer. I came into Spence Field, an expanse of dried grass with views of forever. I climbed through a grove of dwarfed beech trees with a thrasher declaring to the world that this territory was his. On up to the Rocky Knob, then through a corridor of rhododendron to Thunderhead. I stood sweating and short of breath on Thunderhead, watching a black vulture just sailing the wind, rising and falling on the air currents. This is his land and his sky, and I with my human limitations am just a visitor.

On through many ups and downs and areas where the wild hogs had foraged, looking like a rototiller had been there. I saw a wild boar about a mile from Derrick's Bald lean-to. That one was about two feet at the shoulder. These are a cross between introduced black Russian boars and the native variety. The park has a program of relocating the boars as they compete with the shyer deer and bear for feeding territory.

The next day the trail was very much overused and eroded, a spiderweb of exposed roots and loose rock. My feet were hurting, so as an experiment I put on my sneakers. My feet felt so light, they flew down the trail. I made the climb of Clingman's Dome, which is 6,636 feet high, the high point of the Smokies and of the trail. I reached the observation tower all dirty and sweating and was greeted by the fat and smiling tourists who had driven to the top.

From here I began descending through a forest of spruce and fir—their twisted trunks testifying that the breeze isn't always as gentle and refreshing as it was on that day. The trail paralleled the road to Newfound Gap. It was an interesting contrast—the sounds of civilization on one side and the "call of the wild" on the other. On to Newfound Gap tourist parking area, then to Icewater Spring lean-to, a day's hike of 23 miles. Here I met some real fine people, some of them sure to become lifelong friends. I was greeted by Russ, Sue, Barbara, and Ilene.

John Collins.

Then in strolled the living legend of the trail, the man I've been hearing about for two hundred miles. His name is John Collins. A jolly old man of sixty-two years singing Irish songs, shaking hands, and passing out peanuts.

16

Russ, Sue, Barbara, and Ilene with John Collins.

That night was like Christmas with Santa himself, with a fire of fragrant pine boughs in the cozy little shelter filled with songs and laughter, poems and stories shared by this white-bearded man. He recited, "Din! Din! Din!" as the campfire grew dim, and we drifted off to dreams of Annabel Lee. When I got up the next day, John had the fire going and water boiling.

He left before me, but after about five miles I met him sitting under a pine tree like Rumpelstiltskin. We shared a snack of granola, then he moved on as I photographed some flowers and listened to the birds. Next I made my way around a large rocky precipice over the loose cobblestones into the soft light of the pines. I saw a deer about one hundred yards ahead on the trail. We stood looking at each other; then as I moved closer he turned, waved his white flag, and bounded into the brush. I felt guilty about disturbing him in his own land. All I wish to do is borrow this narrow footpath through this garden so I can better appreciate him and his world.

Up on a ridgetop clearing, I heard the drumming of a grouse before I re-entered the spruce. I ascended through tall pines with banks overhanging with rhododendron and blanketed with soft, wet moss that you could dive into. The sun went behind a cloud, and the greens came alive in their own light, then back came the sun glazing all with gold. The air was so cool and moist you could drink it. Again I met my friend John, resting on a bank in the pines. We sat talking about life and shared lunch.

I went on ahead and descended from pines to a deciduous forest of birches, beech, and maples. I was eating violet leaves, as they are rich in vitamin C, when I met two men from Michigan. They turned me on to eating adder's tongue and spring beauties, and with a few field onions, we had a real feast. That night John and I had dandelion greens for supper. Russ, Sue, Barbara, and Ilene caught up, and it was another night of singing and stories. The trail was now becoming more than a walk through nature and solitude—it became a sharing of ourselves and the beauty of the trail with some beautiful people.

Russ and I hiked together to Davenport Gap. Along the way we learned more about wildflowers and more about each other. We got to the lean-to at 4 P.M. and went two and a half more miles to a store, got ice cream and cookies, and had a party back at the lean-to when the girls and John arrived. The next morning we all went to the little store for orange juice and snacks. John hard-boiled some eggs in front of the store, and we all had breakfast. We were now just outside the Great Smoky Mountains National Park and entering the Pisgah National Forest.

This little valley was a utopia of mountain brooks, butterflies, and small farms. We walked down the dirt road together singing songs and dancing in the warmth of the sun and the warmth of friendship. The girls left to see a doctor, as one had foot trouble, and John, Russ, and I went on. We hiked together to Groundhog Creek lean-to, only about ten miles. There the three of us were greeted by three more hikers, Rick, John, and Debbie. We all had supper together, and then went to sleep with rain on the roof.

Pisgah National Forest, North Carolina.

I left alone early in the morning and walked through all the leaves and flowers washed by the rain and hung out to dry in the morning sun. The may-apple looked like a crowded beach of umbrellas. It began raining, and, as I put my rain cover on my pack, Russ and Rick caught up with me. We came to an area where the trail was rerouted this spring though fresh untrodden woods, a pleasant break from the old beaten path. The trail descended on many switch-backs, through blooming tulip and dogwood trees, and the floor was alive with green. The trail was so soft with leaves and rich black soil that it was like walking on a mattress. This section was a real sensual experience. The sun shone through the young leaves, illuminating the vast varieties of green. At least six types of trillium bowed their heads to the sun. Showy orchids in pink and white, dwarf iris in many shades of blue, purple monkshood, violets of all kinds, wild geraniums, and a flurry of shed petals covered the trail. The smells in the air were finer and fresher than in any man-made greenhouse, as all the fragrances blended clean and fresh after the spring rain.

We came down onto Max Patch Road, which was a dirt road through rolling hills of grazing cattle, with little houses tucked within the hollers. We walked past farms and ponds and heard a bobwhite. After about four miles, we reached the Tennessee State line and ascended back into the woods. We saw a male and a female scarlet tanager as we went on through this wilderness wonderland. After 20 miles, we all decided to go the 2.84 more miles into Hot Springs, North Carolina. With thoughts of fresh fruit and a hot shower, we moved on to Deer Park Mountain. Here we saw some pink lady's slippers. Then on down toward the town. At the bottom of the mountain we came to that proverbial pot of gold at the rainbow's end—a hostel run by a Catholic Church with a big sign welcoming trail hikers to stay for free. So off came the pack and I jumped into a nice hot shower—a perfect ending to a perfect day.

I've come about 260 miles in the two and a half weeks I've been out. Only about eighteen hundred to go!

THREE

I left the hostel in Hot Springs early Sunday morning with my friends Russ and Rick, with full packs and full bellies, and said goodbye to John Collins with an embrace and a pledge of lifelong friendship. We walked on through town and into the woods again with the first signs of laurel beginning to bloom. The church bells from the town below bid us farewell. This section of trail skirts along the border of North Carolina's Pisgah Forest and Tennessee's Cherokee National Forest. Stopped for a break at Spring Mountain lean-to amidst pink and white trillium and tall white oak trees. Along the trail were patches of lily of the valley. The trail went on through mixed hardwoods with gardens of wild geranium and patches of budding blueberry bushes for the summer sun to ripen. We descended to and crossed a road at the Tennessee-North Carolina State line and stopped at a gas station for a snack of orange juice and ice cream. Stayed at Little Laurel lean-to.

Monday—I was walking again with Russ and Rick and leapfrogging a couple from Hawaii named Mary and Joe. They are the first Hawaiians to attempt the trail. Joe is 64, and Mary is 60. I wore sneakers again today and was quite comfortable. We identified some new birds. We saw the chestnut-sided warbler and the blue-headed vireo. Again we saw a scarlet tanager. Hiked leisurely on fire roads with many flowering shadbush and dogwood. Saw the first may-apple in flower today. We did some climbing and got a magnificent view off White Rock Cliff of the Tennessee Valley. Most of this part of the trail was wet and rocky, reminding me of the Maine trails.

Mary and Joe, the first Hawaiians to hike the A.T.

Views from White Rocks Cliffs, Tennessee.

We came to a clearing, which was the gravesite of Civil War soldiers. We enjoyed the sun and watched the birds. This section of trail isn't terribly wild but is quite scenic. There is much sign of man—fire roads, jeep roads, and where goes man so go his beer cans. Stopped for the night at Locust Ridge lean-to. The sun was setting on the mountain through the tall tulip trees. The end of the day brought contentment just to be there. We cooked over a fire to save fuel and for the aesthetic value of a campfire.

Sunset and firelight.

At 6:30 this morning, the sun is lighting the sky from behind the mountain. A rooster in a distant valley is summoning all awake and rejoicing in the new day. Closer, a woodpecker is preparing his breakfast, and a crow rallies his troops for a raid on a newly seeded garden. A grouse drums, and a thousand sounds and songs merge in the colors of the rising sun. These are my early-morning outhouse observations. It's nice to have an outhouse on a hill facing east at dawn.

After a quick cold breakfast we pack and leave, hoping to cover some ground today.

The trail went through and around many farms with nice views from cleared mountaintop meadows. We had to cross many barbed wire fences, adding to the challenge of the hike. In some places they constructed stiles for crossing the wire, which were also quite treacherous. There were many steep ascents as the trail went along property boundaries with no room for switchbacks. In the meadow we saw many goldfinches and indigo buntings. We also saw a rose-breasted grosbeak. We finally reached the top of Big Bald—a cleared mountaintop where we sat watching the clouds race over the mountains all around us. We made camp about one mile from the summit in sparse woods full of spring beauties near a spring. Slept under the stars and got a good night's rest, which is impossible in the crowded lean-tos.

Got up under a gray dawn. The rain held off until we were under way, and we stopped to put on rain covers. We stopped at No Business lean-to for lunch. The trail descended steeply to Spivey Gap, then got quite pleasant. The light rain kept me cool while I walked. The trail descended along the Nalichachy River near Erwin, Tennessee. Felt an extreme oppression being in a town breathing lousy air and seeing polluted rivers. Back into the woods—in this low area I saw the first rhododendron blossoms. Always at the end of the day, when you're tired, there's a long steep ascent to the lean-to, and today was no exception. After 19 miles, we arrived at Curly Maple Gap lean-to. I ate everything I could spare, and then went to bed.

Woke to another really cloudy morning. By about 10:30 atop Beauty Spot, it cleared. Beauty Spot is a grassy bald at 4,437 feet with 360-degree views. The wet grass felt cool and refreshing as I lay back in the sun. I noted that the lower back padding on my pack frame was ripped, so I sewed it and applied some ripstop tape. Did some more steep climbing and descending on wet slopes with exposed roots. Once you get the rhythm of the trail, descending is like skiing and you move in perfect harmony with the mountain. We stopped for lunch at Cherry Gap lean-to, and I took a bath in the spring and sat in the sun. Saw two more indigo buntings at Iron Mountain Gap at close range. They put on a real show while we rested. Went on through an overgrown apple orchard and up and down till 6:15 P.M., when we reached High Gap with a nice spring. All around were monkshood in deep blue, and on the trailside was yellow mustard. Had a Durkee instant omelet with cheese, grits, and tomato soup for supper. Just after I ate and went to relax on a well-chosen log with a view, it started raining. So up went the tube tent.

There was thunder and lightning all night long, and it's still raining this morning. We've gotten a little wet, but by evening we will be in Elk Park, North Carolina, where I have to stop for mail.

We climbed, slipped, and sweated over Roan Mountain and got great views of fog. We dripped into Elk Park and to a nice room and split the tab three ways so each of us paid $4.00. We soon made a complete muddy mess of the entire room.

I left the motel early the next morning alone. Russ was staying behind with dysentery, and Rick planned to catch up later when he was able to drag himself out of the comforts of civilization. The first hikers I saw today stood snorting and glaring at me with big brown eyes. The trail wasn't big enough for all of us, so I stood aside and let the seven cows go on their way. Continued on a dirt road to Sunset Orchard—a mountaintop apple orchard all in bloom. The trail was fringed with ferns, and fiddleheads unfurled with new life.

The only bad thing about being first on a trail in the morning is breaking the curtain of webs strung across the path. Came to a pond, and frogs jumped and ducks started to paddle to the center. Apple-blossom petals floated on the water. Suddenly the tranquility was shattered by two German shepherds from a nearby farmhouse. The ducks took off and so did I. Walked out on another road with more farms and more dogs. Smells of bacon and eggs came from a farmhouse, and an old horse stood warming itself in the morning sun.

Rick caught up, and we hiked through rolling pastures full of flowers and saw two blackbirds. Stopped at a fire tower and watched with envy the soaring of a hawk. From the tower the trail descended though a little paradise with a stream flowing through rhododendrons. We startled a deer on the hill above us. She stopped and looked at us, and we looked back at her. This time the deer didn't run. We just greeted each other as fellow wanderers in the wilderness. She made me feel that I am no longer an intruder here. We stopped at Coon Den Falls and played on the hanging vines and in the water.

Stretched across the trail in the sun was a four-foot black snake. We watched with wonder as this amazing creature moved gracefully off the trail. We descended to a large stream and went wading again. We walked in the cool air along the river through pink and white rhododendron down to some real high falls. Stayed at Laurel Fork lean-to and watched the sun sink into a gap between the mountains. Here there was a father-and-son team, Rick and Dick, from Michigan; Joel, my young smiling friend I met way back in Georgia on Blood Mountain; Sally; and a big guy who snored all night.

Got up to yet another rainy morning. Saw two yellow lady's slippers. Pink lady's slippers are like long-necked spectators along the trail. Fire pinks brightened the path under pink and white laurel and rhododendron and orange azalea. Came to a ridge over Wilbur Lake. Descended and crossed a bridge over the river. We watched the butterflies below chasing their reflections on water. About 5 P.M., after some steep climbing, we explored a worn side trail in hopes of finding a spring. Better yet, we found a cabin that had four bunks with mattresses and a potbellied stove, with a picnic table and a sign welcoming hikers outside. Without further ado, the guys and I each took a bath. We sat around the picnic table eating and waiting for our nightly rainstorm to come in. At sunset the rain began, and a whip-poor-will started calling.

On Tuesday morning the birds' singing told me the sun was up even though the deceiving darkness at the cabin didn't let on. I sat up and ate my oatmeal and grits before the others got up. I listened to the wind causing waves of showers to fall from the misty columns of tulip, maple, oak, and beech.

Using my hiking stick I fend off the wild rose, blackberry brambles, and poison ivy that hang out into the trail to snare my bare legs. It also comes in handy to break the spiderwebs that seek to entangle me. As the shadbush petals flurry down onto the trail, and the dogwood petals begin to follow suit, a whole new wave of summer growth is taking its place in the sun. The spring greens turn deeper and darker. The rich fragrance of mayapple permeates the wet, heavy air as I walk along a narrow, breezy ridgetop with views of stark white fog in both directions. Shy little bellworts show their pale yellow flowers while bold buttercups glow with glory. Mayapple blossoms peek out from under their parasols.

Came upon a lone grave in the clearing decorated with violets and geraniums. The grave marked the last lonely mountaintop resting spot for Uncle Nick Grindstaff with an epitaph that read: "Lived alone, suffered alone, died alone. December 26, 1855–July 22, 1923." It might have been his old cabin we stayed in that night. Went on past a lean-to and found a nice shelter in the rocks along the ridge.

Got up early and hiked the gently descending ridge to the Tennessee-Virginia State line, then into Damascus, Virginia. Here I met my old friend Jeff, who had taken a vacation from the trail. He had a room here, so Rick and I sneaked in.

It's now May 14—exactly one month since I left Amicalola Falls State Park, in Georgia, and 430 miles from the beginning of the trail. From here it's 320 miles to Shenandoah National Park.

FOUR

Again I leave behind the comforts of civilization to continue my journey. I can still feel the effects of my stay in Damascus, Virginia, as my stomach complains. It's a cloudy Thursday, May 15, as I walk down the road to where the trail leaves man's world and re-enters the dreamy wilderness world. The woods stand stark still, the silence broken only occasionally by the short, swift flight of a towhee. All waiting in a moment of silence—the calm before the storm, then the rain begins, and the cool drops bring relief from the oppressive heavy air.

R ick caught up with me, and we walked along a beautifully graded trail above and along a river through Laurel Gap. We met Jeff at the gate on the fence line of land owned by Jerry Dean. We met old Jerry doing his chores around his farm. With a quote of the Golden

Rule—"Do unto others . . ."—he offered us the use of one of his sheds for lunch and to get out of the now heavy rain. We ended up staying there along with other hikers. A girl named Betsey, from Florida, had been there a week helping plant peppers on the farm. She told us of some of Jerry's neighbors. Mrs. McQueen in Damascus is descended from Davey Crockett, and in a cabin down the road a spell is Mrs. Boone—from the Daniel Boone family. We left our little shanty at about 7:30 Friday morning. The trail was well graded, then became rougher in some new sections on wet hillsides. On and up the steep muddy trail to Whitetop Mountain. With each step forward, I slipped back six inches in the mud. The name Whitetop is appropriate for a couple reasons. The summit was covered in a crown of clouds that seemed to have snowed lacy fringed phacelia. One moment I looked up and saw Jeff silhouetted against the sky atop the castlelike rocky peak, then like a vision from the past, he disappeared in the fog.

Moving on we had an all-natural lunch next to a stream. We feasted on ramps, adder's tongue, spring beauties, and fiddleheads. I'd like to see Euell Gibbons top that menu. Our feast was cut short by the cold rain, and we moved down the beautiful misty trail. On through a pasture, dodging cow pies in the fog, and into flower-flurried woods to Deep Gap lean-to, a real paradise with ramps for munchies and fringed phacelia all around. Rick, Jeff, and I meditated together in the lean-to, and afterwards our spontaneous laughter filled the woods

We woke again Saturday morning to rainy skies, rolled over, and slept until 7:30, when I got up and shivered into my damp clothes and soggy boots. I figured the only way to get warm was to get moving, so on I went toward Mt. Rogers. I ascended on through the time machine back into springtime. High on the mountain, the trees and flowers were still await-ing their time to flourish in the sun.

On into the hush of the pines—walking silently on a cloud of soft needles. Everywhere the intense green of life glows in the fog. An infinite variety of shapes appear in the mist, and all the trees, the tall and the fallen, wear a living carpet of moss.

Mountaintop Meditations

To let the forest get inside without thinking about what is happening.

Letting the mind go clear, resting in the enclosure of awe-some silence.

Held penetrated, invaded, until the odor of the needles and moist earth, the gentle sound of a falling cone or a singing bird speaks from deep inside you.

On to the summit of Mt. Rogers, the highest point in Virginia, 5,729 feet. I came out of the pines and was met by a gust of windblown fog, and went on through Rhododendron Gap and over Pine Mountain to lunch at Old Orchard lean-to. Wendy and Sue from Massachusetts were there also.

They had seen three wild ponies during their hikes. These ponies belong to a farmer who lets them graze in the mountain meadows and rounds them up each year. If I saw one, I'd round him up myself and let him carry my pack.

From here we did some quick, wet miles and landed in Hurricane campsite. This was a state-maintained park for "regular" campers. It even had restrooms with a hot shower, a real luxury after a few days of fog and rain. After a good long shower, I started to set up my campsite. After much thought and debate, I decided to slit my tube tent up the middle, making a large tarp. I strung this over my rope and held the sides down with rocks and had myself a large, livable dry shelter. I climbed in and listened to the rain and spring peepers.

I woke up at 5:45 to a great surprise. I don't know whether my prayers were answered by God or my gripes were overheard by neighboring campers. In addition to my stuff bag of food, hanging in a tree was a plastic bag that contained four oranges, two tomatoes, six eggs, and cheese. "Mine is not to question why," so I ate. Like the flowers and the trees, we are taken care of.

I'm feeling very high this morning as I walk with all my flower friends along the trail. Each different plant, each a different shape, size, color—each an experiment in the design of living— each striving for and evolving toward some unknown perfect form—each springing from the earth reaching for the sun—each moment of discovery is part of our aliveness with that life which forever impels us to go further, continuing our own evolution.

On past a squirrel's tabletop scattered with acorns from his lunch and though rolling hills with grazing cows and calves running in the rain. Followed a dirt road, grazing on red clover, through a muddy barnyard onto a paved road into Teas, Virginia. We met Sue and Wendy sitting on an old sofa in front of what used to be a store, eating peanut butter sandwiches. Rick and I hitched into the next town with a store and feasted on oatmeal cookies, apples, oranges, and peanut butter and apple butter sandwiches.

We got back and walked the ugliest part of the trail yet. We went up through the mud on a road made by a bulldozer to a sand and gravel pit. The mud on my boots made them weigh about ten pounds apiece. On up an ungraded rocky trail, tripping and slipping on the loose rock. I finally made it to Killinger Creek lean-to and ran back to help Rick, who had developed shin splints. To top off a perfect afternoon, the water was unfit for drinking without treating it with halazone tablets. This was the worst lean-to yet because of its closeness to a road and to people. The wallboards were torn off for firewood, and beer cans were all over. We cleaned it up and made it home for a night. I lay awake late, listening to the bizarre sounds of owls, whip-poor-wills, and little creatures running back and forth in front of the shelter.

Another cloudy morning and a nice descent though farms and flowers on a muddy path over a fence into a pasture of horses, ponies, and cows. The herd of cattle separated to let me pass, as I came upon a road lined with phlox and iris. On past a farmhouse with a web of wisteria and a pen of peacocks, past a hillside of baaing sheep. We came out to a road with a restaurant. I had a quick tomato juice and left the others behind. I went on under Interstate 81, through a chicken farm, and onto a dirt road. The road narrowed as I danced through stinging nettle. Finally, the cow tracks gave way to deer tracks, and I re-entered the woods. Pink geraniums, yellow and orange azalea, and a singing stream greeted me. After a few steep climbs I was on a sunny ridge with yellow star grass, fire pink, lousewort, buttercups, chickweed, geraniums, and violets. I descended very steeply into a valley crisscrossed by brooks and took a bath, then washed my hair and clothes in the stream flowing through the rhododendron. I ascended slowly up Walker Mountain to Walker Mountain lean-to.

I put all my stuff out to dry on the first sunny warm afternoon in a week, then went up to the nearby fire tower to see what Virginia looks like without clouds. To the north were farms—in all directions, mountains. The mooing of cows in the valley could barely be heard; up here I was serenaded by the music of the wind. Went back to the shelter to see if the others had caught up—no sign. I had some soy milk and moved along the ridge. I watched the sun sinking, pouring out more and more colors until it disappeared behind the mountains. With a half-moon overhead, I found a suitable campsite among the mayapple, strung my tarp, and went to bed.

The still and darkness of the night faded into morning, and light brought me back from my sleep. As I sat up, the air began to stir with the morning change in temperature. The sun had not risen over the ridge as I packed. I sat facing east and meditated in the first rays.

Everything glistens with dew as I walk directly into the rising sun. The air is alive with birdsongs and the sounds of sheep, cattle, dogs, and roosters. A grouse drums in the distance.

A rose-breasted grosbeak sings his treetop morning chant as the air warms.

I stopped to enjoy the sun, the breeze, and the view off Monster Rock. Here and there was a farmhouse or a barn, and cows and sheep dotted the green valley. Sheets of haze laced between the rolling hills. The air was so sweet and fresh—and I was so high. On past Monster Rock lean-to to Walker Mountain Lookout and restaurant. I got four glasses of orange juice and a pair of sunglasses. From the restaurant I ascended gradually on a dirt road with views on my right. This road went for eight miles with buzzards circling overhead, waiting for me to drop in my tracks. Finally I was off the dirt road and into the woods to Turkey Gap lean-to for lunch.

As I passed on through groves of trillium, it was hard to believe how many colors I saw—every shade from pure white to fuchsia, from pink to purple. Through a forest of interrupted fern up to my elbows. I felt like I could lie back and float along on the fragrance of the lilies of the valley, which now formed the forest greenery. I got to High Rock lean-to and crashed for about one and a half hours after a twenty-mile day. I got some energy together and walked to the rocky overlook beneath the fire tower. The rocks were speckled with pale green lichen, and the pastels of the sunset merged with the haze in the valley. In the sky were wisps of color directed back toward that single point in the west. The deep greens of the valley turned to blues in the haze and changing sky. The colors became more and more intense. I raised my arms in praise—the wind rose and carried me along like a hawk into the sunset. Cows lowed, and lights came on in the valley below, and a whip-poor-will chorus began that would last all night.

Trillium.

Rob from Massachusetts showed up, followed by a stray dog. This boy is sixteen, in high school, carrying on correspondence courses while hiking. He has three ongoing chess matches and reads Greek fluently. He also wears braces on both legs and is still doing the whole trail. We climbed the tower together and watched the remaining colors fade into the blues and grays at night.

The next morning I fed the dog sardines, and he became mine. I named him Tower, and he followed on my heels down the trail, through cow pastures into Crandon, Virginia. I bought him some dog food and myself a cantaloupe, bananas, and grape juice. Rob caught up, and we walked on through farms on dirt roads. We came to a bridge over a nice, deep river and went swimming, of course. On and on down the road, until finally I was back to the woods. Rob fell behind at another store. I took a bath in Dismal Creek and went on. I stopped to taste the air filled with scents of pine, azalea, and dogwood on an old logging road carpeted with green grass studded with buttercups.

Went on through sweet-smelling pines and cherry all in blossom to the blue-blaze trail to Wapiti lean-to. I saw about 30 tiger swallowtail and black swallowtail butterflies all together on a little sandy beach on Dismal Creek. It seemed like they were splashing from a waterfall. Wendy and Sue, and Rob and Tom from Florida, all arrived here later.

I got up early, 5:30, and fed Tower some more dog food, then said good-bye to my canine partner. He's now traveling with Rob. I got started in the cool morning air and walked on through with delights on either side like gay wings and white stonecrop. Continued on down the steep, muddy descent into Pearisburg, Virginia. I stopped at the post office, then went to the nearest fruit stand. I bought half a watermelon, sat on a peach basket on the sidewalk, and slobbered it all down. Just as I finished my feast, Len Darcy, Ilene Dunn, and two other people from my hometown of Cheshire greeted me. They are on their way to start the trail. I hitched a ride in search of a Catholic Church hostel I'd heard about from other hikers. Father Charles greeted me at the Holy Family Church. He is from Hamden, Connecticut, and is related to the Priest family in Cheshire. After taking a shower and washing my clothes, I planted a flower garden at the church. Later I went to the chapel with the father, listened to Gregorian chants, and meditated. Other hikers arrived. We had a supper of hot dogs and beans outside.

The next morning I drove with Father Charles into Blacksburg and went to a hiking supply store and a bookstore. I dropped off my boots to get them resoled there in preparation for another 1,500 miles of walking.

Father Charles and I became very close in my short stay in this area.

While walking along, I've been assessing the personal benefits I've been deriving from my journey. I feel very lucky to have this beautiful world to view and a healthy body to take me through it. This brings my thoughts to the future—will these natural areas prevail through time? My thoughts also go out to those who are physically and mentally unable to get out to see the wonders nature has to offer. So I've decided to make this my own personal walkathon if I can get some good-hearted people to back me. If any business, group, or individual in Cheshire would like to make a pledge of any amount per mile I walk and donate it to any charity they wish, maybe we can make this world even better.

FIVE

As I prepare to leave Pearisburg and Holy Family Church, I know I'll be saying goodbye to a good person, Father Charles, a fine man of God and a true friend of mine. We part with an embrace, and I walk on toward town to pick up my re-soled boots and to stop at the post office.

I n town I met Art from the church with Rick, Jeff, and Joel in the car. They gave me a ride to the trail, and we said more goodbyes. Back on the trail again, I was soon treated to a bunch of wild strawberries. As I munched, I watched a garter snake slide through the weeds. After an arduous ascent up the steep, rocky hill under power lines, I finally left civilization behind and re-entered the woods. Back to my old friends, geraniums, trilliums, maidenhair fern, rue, and the cool ridgetop breeze. I came into a long mountaintop field scattered with mountain myrtle and pink and white chickweed. I stopped here and had a snack of milk and granola. As I ate I was circled by six vultures and two crows that flew within 20 feet of me.

A dark cloud came by, giving me a much needed shower, and then moved on, leaving me with sunshine. I caught up with Tom from Florida and Bo and walked the ridge, then descended through rhododendron to a spring. We stopped for a drink and were driven on by the blackflies. We descended on a rocky path along a stream flowing over moss-covered rocks in a dark jungle of rhododendron. Followed the stream down to Pine Swamp shelter in a grove of tall tulip trees. Jeb from North Carolina showed up, and we all ate some milkweed I'd picked earlier.

I left early the next morning while the others slept, and hiked along a stream. After a short time the trail crossed the stream in a wide, deep area. I put on my sneakers and stepped into the swift, cold water. I managed to get to the other side without slipping on the algae-covered rocks. After that refreshing dip, I went through a swampy area full of rhododendrons and up through hemlocks and oak, with an occasional holly tree. On past Bailey lean-to on a dirt road, I stopped for a lunch of rice cakes and honey, and was soon joined by a family of sightseers. After having to snap five pictures of them I decided to move on.

I met more people out for Memorial Day strolls before finally setting back on the narrow trail again. The spicy smell of azalea was like walking into a cedar chest. On down a two-mile steep descent to War Branch lean-to, where I took a bath and watched a white-tail deer drinking in a sunny pool upstream. A sign on the lean-to told of a massive relocation of the trail ahead. Some private land had been closed to hikers, and the trail was being rebuilt around this section. The sign suggested getting a ride around, as the trail had not been completed. I came down to a dirt road and walked about three miles to a paved road where I begged a ride from a guy building his dream house in the mountains. It so happened that he has a brother who lives on Patton Drive in Cheshire. He gave me a ride to the town of Maggie, which consisted of a country store. Again I lucked out, as some people in the store were going to the place where I wanted to pick up the trail. They gave me a ride to Catawba Mountain, where I gave their little boy a bird's nest I found for his birthday and said goodbye.

With thunder crashing, I walked about one and a half miles to Boy Scout lean-to. Just as I arrived so did the rain—welcome relief from the 90-degree heat. With the music of the rain on the roof, I decided to make some music of my own. I got out the harmonica I bought in Pearisburg and struggled with "Hot Cross Buns."

Got up at 6:00 the next morning and took my time getting started. I walked off into the fog cooled by the rain off the trees. The trail was crawling with fluorescent orange-red efts, the juvenile form of the newt salamander. Out of the eerie green mist three invisible ravens flew, cawing overhead. The twisted dark trunks of the ridgeline trees were silhouetted against the fog. Bedstraw and burrs clung to my socks as I went through the narrow, wet path being drenched by the brushing bushes. I stood on a rocky cliff gazing into the vast foggy nothingness. Sounds came out of the valley below, but I could see nothing. I was looking now with my ears— they came alive to make up for my lack of vision. By the sounds I formed a picture of the valley below: to the right were farms and towns, to the left silent mountains.

Wet webs hung waving in the wind like nets on a fishing boat. Went on in the fog over Tinker Mountain and down into Cloverdale as the sun burned through. At Fullhardt Knob lean-to, I met Harry from Florida and the "Cinci Boys," three guys from Cincinnati. We sat and watched a thunderstorm swirl on the treetops and hammer us with hailstones. Then as quickly as it came, it left us to watch the sunset and the first stars appearing in the deepening blue of the evening sky.

Got started at about 7 A.M., chewing a birch twig as I walked. Along the trail were Virginia spiderwort ranging in hue from fuchsia to blue to deep purple. Bowman's root reached its spiderlike white blossoms into the trail. Tall, long-necked turkey head burned like a candle through the sparse woods. A wood turtle made his way slowly up the trail. On past sweet fern and budding laurel. Blueberry bushes all in flower—some heavy with green fruit. Solomon's seal had changed from bud to hanging bellflowers. As I walked, I carried my hiking staff in front to break the webs, one disadvantage of being an early bird on the trail. The trail crossed the Blue Ridge Parkway twice and paralleled it for a while, then up on the Blue Ridge with the flowing fuchsia flowers of rhododendron on all sides and above. Staying at Bablette Gap lean-to tonight. Had a dinner of poke "sallet," which tasted like asparagus.

Another 7 A.M. start crossing the Blue Ridge Parkway again. Had a feast of strawberries. A long, steep climb, but the sweat was wiped from my brow by the cool breeze, and the strain in my mind and body was replaced by the sweet mixture of scents from rhododendron, laurel, and flame azalea. I found myself standing in a dream—flowers so full—scents all flowing in the morning breeze. A carpet of soft emerald green moss rolled out before me as I walked down through this fantastic fusion of fuchsia and green. Brambles of maple-leafed viburnum tinged with pink lined the ridgetop trail softened by pine needles. The sun shining through the trees illuminated the white laurel lanterns. I stopped on the ridgetop, took off my pack and boots, and sat playing my harmonica. I'm afraid I'm no competition for the rose-breasted grosbeak above me, so I put my harmonica away to listen to the music of the woods.

Moved on and took a bath at Cove Branch shelter with black, blue, tiger, and zebra swallowtail butterflies dancing in the sun. The afternoon's hike wasn't quite so easy and beautiful. Up, up, up, and up some more through nettles and sweltering heat. Harry caught up, and we got to Cornelius Creek lean-to at about 5 P.M.

On the trail at 7, and the rain started at 8. I danced over rocks, dodging nettles through the rain with heavy, wet boots. Got to Thunderhill lean-to just as the rain stopped. Had some tea and honey and moved on, traveling very fast. The beauty of yesterday's rhododendron gave way to the biting sting of today's nettle. Some long, hard, wet climbs on overgrown trail. Stopped at Marble Spring lean-to to wring out my socks. Getting eaten by blackflies to complement the itch of the nettles. Got to Matt Creek shelter and was greeted by about fourteen boys on a school trip filing into the lean-to. Took a bath in the stream and found room in the crowded shelter.

Left Jefferson National Forest at the James River and went to the post office and store in Snowden, Virginia. Entered the George Washington National Forest at Goshen Creek with the smell of honeysuckle and whorled loosestrifes. Stopped at John Hollow lean-to and said goodbye to Harry.

I hiked on seeing no one, no footsteps marred the moist trail—the only steps were my own, the only voices those of the birds and the wind. The trail was very mellow as I talked to the clouds and walked in the warm sun and easterly breeze. All along the trail were laurel, rhododendron, and young hickory. I stopped and watched the bees in the rhododendron, leg pouches heavy with pollen—everything they need lies in the beauty of these flowers. Columbine, orange and yellow, like bloomered circus clowns, did acrobatics in the breeze. A mama grouse put on her "dance of deceit" as I walked by her nest. First she took off through the brush screaming and faking a broken wing to lure me away from the nest. After that failed, she valiantly challenged me with neck feathers and tail unfurled and beak ready to strike. I assured her of my honorable intentions and moved on.

Steep climbs to Rocky Knole, up Siles Knob, and on to Bluff Mountain. On down a new trail to Punchbowl lean-to with a pond full of salamanders and chirping frogs. Took a bath in the pond and emerged smelling like a frog. Here I met Rick and Ernie from Maryland. The spring peepers, tree toads, and bullfrogs were so loud at night that I had to put toilet paper in my ears.

I awoke the next morning with a bullfrog foghorn and a shroud of fog over the pond. A bobwhite sang in the meadow. Left just as the sun broke through in the virgin forest of hemlock, beech, and oak overlooking a terraced stream. On through a hay field full of strawberries headed toward the Peddle Reservoir. The trail was studded with turquoise chips of robins' eggs. Partridgeberry and Christmas fern lined the trail. On up from the reservoir and cool stream to Balk Knob and Cole Mountain. The trail was invisible in the fog on the bald mountaintops, making it very difficult to follow. Met Stacey and Helen from Staten Island also wandering in the fog.

We made it to Wiggin Spring shelter.

Got started in the morning just as the rain stopped. Donned my rain chaps in an attempt to keep the water out of my boots and the nettles out of my legs. Ernie caught up with me as I tried to determine where the mountains stopped and the clouds began. Moved on over Rocky Mountain and up Maine Top Mountain, then on to the Priest Mountain shelter.

The clouds clear, and I sit on a rock in the wind to watch the sun set. The day seems so long until these last few moments of sunlight that pass so quickly behind distant mountains.

*I watch the world turn as the last rays sink into the cool
mountains.*

    Shimmering oak trees turn from green to gold
    Wind telling tales ages old
    Of the setting sun and clouds in the sky
    I'll hear it all before I die.

Got up at 5:30, listened to the birds and left in the rising sun. I headed
due east over the Priest into the rising sun. I stepped out on a rocky overview
of the Virginia Mountains, intensely green in the blue sky and bright sun
with the air washed clean in yesterday's rain. Everywhere birds were singing; everything pulsed with freshness and life. Descended the Priest crossing
many cascading streams through air filled with honeysuckle. Took a bath
in the Type River, then crossed the bridge and began climbing the Three
Ridges. Picked some poke for a special lunch for everyone and cooked it at
Harpers Creek lean-to. Moved on with Rick and Ernie to Laurel Spring. I set
up my tarp and watched the lightning dance in the sky all around.

Got up early and blazed on down the wet, difficult trail to Rock Fish
Gap. Here I met up with Jeff from Syracuse again. After a sundae at Howard
Johnson's, we moved on to the Shenandoah National Park. After crossing
two fences in the woods, we entered a large mountaintop cow pasture full of
sunshine and strawberries. Re-entered the woods through laurel and rhododendron on beautiful, wide graded trails. Columbine, larkspur, and Virginia
spiderwort lined the trail. Hiked to Sawmill Run lean-to and camped in the
woods below. In the park it is prohibited to camp within sight of the shelters
and the trail in an attempt to restore overused areas. Cooked up some more
poke, then hung our food in a tree out of a bear's reach.

Left at 7 and ascended the ridge through laurel. Clumps of mistletoe hung in the trees. The fragrance of locust blossoms filled the air. Moved on to the Loft Mountain campsite and took a hot shower. We got a nice site on a hillside and slept in the sun. Later we washed our clothes and got some fruit in the camp store. It's like the Garden of Eden, with deer walking all around free and fearless. Flowers and strawberries everywhere. I met two girls who offered to mail cookies and bread to upcoming towns. That will be a nice break from rice cakes and peanut butter. We hung around in the sun all morning, then the clouds told us to move on to better shelter. On through locust, ash, and oak with fringed phacelia at their feet. The dry smell of hay-scented fern rode the breeze. Many deer and bear trails criss-crossed through the summer grapes.

The trail was wide and grassy, and the trees were sparse. This area was once cleared by settlers for fields and orchards. The warm sun was able to reach my body as I walked. This area is "succeeding" from pasture back to woodland. The locust and cherry are gradually being replaced by oak, ash, and hickory. The trail was beautifully maintained—the underbrush was mowed away from the trail, and switchbacks made the walk gentle. Concrete pillars with engraved metal bands marked intersections and distance.

On through the tunnel of witch hazel to a trail softened by white pine needles. Stayed at Pinefield lean-to and wished on a thousand stars and thanked ten thousand for the wishes I've been granted.

On down the trail with more deer tracks than human. Mountain myrtle, lupines, apple, and blackberry, all in bloom. Sat up on High-top Mountain and watched the shadows of clouds race across the sea of weaving trees. Went on to Big Meadow campsite, and Jeff amused himself by setting up our tarps, forming a huge tent. Spent the night and left at 8 A.M., while through the campsite, the cool breeze was full of the smell of bacon and eggs as the campers arose. Picked up the trail and walked through black and yellow birch.

🌲

The Shenandoahs—each birdsong joyously celebrating life, and each flower a smiling friend, each free deer and animal brothers as we watch seasons unfold like a holy book, each verse full of eternal wisdom, and between each line, universal love. I've just completed the one hundred miles of trail in the park and the 867 miles of trail since Springer Mountain.

White-tailed deer in the Shenandoahs.

SIX

A fter hiking the 104 miles of the Shenandoah National Park, I was met by my parents for a brief interlude. It was a dream come true seeing them—and enjoying all the good food they brought with them. We took a sightseeing tour of Skyline Drive—the second time I've driven in two months. With them they brought a letter of my acceptance to the Peace Corps and an invitation to work with them in the Philippines. After much thought I decided to reject this offer and continue on the path I'm following. After a couple of fine days of wining and dining, rest and relaxing, my parents left me off on the trail at Gravel Springs Gap, the last place that the trail crosses Skyline Drive in the park.

After saying goodbye to my parents, I descended on a fire road to Chester Gap and said goodbye to the park. The trail followed a road for about two miles to an old Confederate training camp now owned by the Smithsonian Institution as a study area for exotic animals. Here I saw some sights I never expected to see on the Appalachian Trail. I cleaned my contacts and rubbed my eyes, but they were telling the truth. Before me were giraffes and zebras, llamas and beavers. On up to Mosby lean-to and took a bath in the nice spring. Stayed here alone and watched the evening turn to night as the last golden rays of the sun reflected on all of creation, and my mind reflected on the beauty of nature and the nature of life.

Up at 5, did my exercises, and meditated as the sky brightened into the new day. Left camp at about 7 A.M. and descended a rutted dirt road full of leaves, out to a paved road to Linden. Stopped at the post office, which was right on the trail. Here I received a big batch of cookies, pretzels, and tea from Judy, a girl from Vermont I had met in the Shenandoahs. I also received a book from my friend Darien. The energy and love from these people gives me the strength to go on. On along a country road with the fragrance of yellow and white honeysuckle, light blue chicory, and sweet pea and the call of the bobwhite. On into the woods happily enjoying the mellow sunny morning eating cookies and wild strawberries until I ran into a No Trespassing sign. Again, the trail ahead was closed by the owner.

This land had been bought by the Blue Ridge Development Company and was now closed to hikers. So out through a hay field full of strawberries and onto a dirt road. I lucked out and caught a ride from a telephone repairman all the way to Snickers Gap. The trail followed the road all this way, about 20 miles. We went by Weather Mountain, which I learned from the driver is a "secret" government installation connected to Washington by tunnel where the President goes in times of emergency. I think my friend saw too many James Bond movies. Just past this is the site of a T.W.A. plane crash. The treetops were sheared off as if with a chain saw.

I picked up the trail at Snickers Gap and was finally back in the woods. After an ascent on a rocky trail, it was flat ridgetop walking all the way to Wilson's Gap lean-to. The ridge continued to Harpers Ferry, West Virginia. This little historic town is the site of the Appalachian Trail Conference headquarters. I walked through time past Stonewall Jackson's headquarters and Jefferson's Rock, with a view of the Potomac and Shenandoah Rivers merging and flowing to the sea. On to the trail conference and, on the front porch, I met my dear friend Tim again, for the last time on the trail. He received a call to follow a new path. I went inside, and there were Rick and Ernie, also preparing to leave the trail— but just for a week's vacation. I signed the register and moved on with Tim to an American Youth Hostel on the outskirts of town. Tim and I meditated and talked on into the night, and when morning came I bid farewell to a beautiful, real friend.

From the hostel the trail went across a bridge and down the old Tote Path running between a canal and the Shenandoah River. This path was once used by horses to tote barges down the canal. Now it's used by bikers and hikers.

As I wandered down the path shaded by sycamore and elm trees, painted turtles splashed off sunny logs into the murky canal. A water snake slid from a puddle into the canal, streaking a path through the film of duckweed. The whole canal became a still, solid green carpet that looked like you could walk on it. This green entirety was occasionally slashed by the swirling tail of a large carp.

On into Maryland and up the steep ascent to Waverton's Cliffs with a view of the rivers below. Walked on easy trail to Gathland State Park, with many Civil War relics. Sat around in the sun for one and a half hours, then moved on up a rocky trail through pastel laurel to a fire tower. The trail led from woods to paved road to the South Mountain Inn, where I stopped for blueberry pie and orange sherbet. From here I moved on to Washington Monument State Park, where I filled up on wild strawberries. I walked into the park and took off my pack at a camping area, but before I even got my boots off I got an invitation to dinner, which of course I accepted. So I ate and talked with the Pressleys, an older couple from Washington. Started getting dark, so I set up my tarp beneath the tall tulip tree.

Got up early the next morning, walked through the park and past the Washington Monument. The trail from here wasn't exactly a wilderness footpath—I crossed I-70 and Route 40, followed the highway, and hiked on eroded trails. I took a side trail to Annapolis Rocks, bathed in a spring, and sat on some rocks in the sun watching a group of rock climbers. Went on and had another feast of strawberries and sat in Antietam Creek. On up to High Rock Cliffs with views of a valley full of farms off in the haze. The sun was still warm as I watched its colors fade into the clouds on the horizon and reflect off scattered barn roofs in the valley below. Set up my tarp on a grassy area and spent the night.

Continued on early the next morning to the town of Pen-Mar and across the border into Pennsylvania. Crossed the Mason-Dixon Line and the halfway point of the trail. Went on past Antietam Creek lean-to up to Chimney Rocks. The view was fogged in, so I moved on quickly and went on past Mt. Alto Sanatorium into Caledonia State Park within Michaux State Forest. I again caught up to Jeff from New York and Ken from Philly. We hitched into Gettysburg and filled up on Breyers ice cream, and Jeff and I went back to spend the night at Caledonia State Park.

Climbed out of the park, past Quarry Gap lean-to to the ridge through Pine Grove Furnace State Park, took a swim in the pond, and climbed back on the ridge. We walked past giant pyramid anthills five feet high and ten feet around, full of red ants, then on to Allen, followed by another 20-mile road section. On we trekked through pretty dairy farms and their rock barns with Pennsylvania Dutch hex signs through the Cumberland Valley, then back into the woods with a hard rocky climb to the ridge. Stayed at Thelma Marks lean-to.

The trail continued along the rocky ridge with a few hazy views of the Susquehanna River. On down into the town of Duncannon on the river. Jeff and I slept in the cemetery there, a very peaceful place to celebrate life.

We took our time getting started, went to the post office and grocery store, then on down the Appalachian sidewalk, cross-town, and across the Susquehanna River. Here in man's world again—the mountain breeze replaced by the smoggy smell of cars and trucks, the songs of the birds replaced by the honking of horns, my feet were no longer caressed by the soft forest floor—instead they were scorched by the fiery furnace of the sidewalk.

Finally out of this man-made inferno, and again the gentle rays of the sun filtered through the leaves of tall tulip and oak trees. Back to the taste of a cool, sweet mountain spring, another healing breath of pure mountain air filling my tortured lungs, the gentle breeze wisping away the thought of what was behind. On the ridge I looked out on the world below—valleys tamed and cuddled beneath a patchwork quilt of farms. The tall, straight columns of tulip, oak, and maple welcomed us into the halls of their divine temple. Fuchsia raspberry flowers brightened the trailside, and all the lush summer plants were trying to "out-green" each other.

Walking along the wide trail, I was suddenly stopped by a vision in the corner of my eye, on the side of the trail, in the exact spot of my next footstep. A shape and color not quite like the trail appeared. With my foot raised and in motion for my next footstep, I was pulled backward by some instinctive force and into automatic reverse I went, with the word "rattler" forming on my lips. There, in front of me lay a three-foot timber rattle-snake with his camouflage of browns, yellows, greens, and golds making him almost invisible. I watched in fascination this creature so feared by so many. His magnificent muscular body, chiseled head, and stony strong expression filled me with great respect and admiration for this serpentine sculpture. As all of creation reacts to the vibration of love, so, too, did this supposedly awesome rattler. Never did he shake his tail—no sign of aggres-sion was made, though my leg was only six inches from his fangs. Perhaps the snake's reputed aggressive behavior is just his natural reaction to the hate, fear, and anger directed toward him by narrow-minded humans. This is the first live venomous snake I've seen on the trail. Perhaps these killer snakes prefer to feed on rodents and insects. Contrary to popular opinion, snakes don't eat people. If people could look at all things in nature and see the divine design behind each and every creature, perhaps they could over-come their fear. It's this fear that makes them alter and hide from nature instead of living and loving it.

Stopped at the top of a mountain and had a lunch of rice cakes, peanut butter, honey, and raisins, all sent to me by the fine people at the Cheshire Emporium, my hometown health food grocery. The next morning I left the Shaffer lean-to and covered myself with Ole Time Woodsman Fly Dope hiker's perfume to ward off the mosquitoes and stumbled one-half mile down a rock slide to the spring below. Came up, meditated under my mos-quito netting, and ate supper with Jeff. As we sat eating, a cottontail rabbit cautiously came within ten feet of us. We talked and read as the sun turned from yellow to orange and disappeared into the blue of the mountains. I set up my tarp to keep the dew off my sleeping bag and went to sleep. We were awakened in the middle of the night by the scream of a bobcat out for a midnight snack.

Up again at 5 A.M. to a beautiful morning. Got chased off early by mosquitoes after a quick breakfast of granola. On down the narrow ridge through tall chestnut and black oaks. The summer foliage blocked most of the views, and the trail was rough and rocky. The steep descent brought us out to Route 325. Just beyond the road was Clark Creek, where I went for a swim, then on to a lunch stop at beautiful Rausch Gap shelter amidst huge fir trees. The shelter was stone with a log roof. Outside, there was a round table with a tree in the middle and a big fireplace. Lots of dirt roads from here and onto the highway under Route 81 across a river, then a climb back to the ridge. Set up tarp by a spring for the night.

On over more rocks and more dirt roads through Pennsylvania State Game Lands. Off the road again to Nay's lean-to for a light lunch, then up again on more rocky trails with some good views of Port Clinton. Walking down the streets, I felt like a celebrity. All the people on their front porches waved and stopped us to talk. Each and every one told us of the church pavilion that is available for hikers to sleep in. All of them talk with a beautiful German accent and a beautiful smile. We went on to the pavilion, where we met Jeb from North Carolina again. Jeff and I bought a jar of homemade chowchow—a mixture of garden vegetables and watermelon in sweet and sour sauce—from a little old-fashioned candy store.

We left the next morning and proceeded into the best day yet in Pennsylvania and a beautiful welcome for the summer season. We left at 7:30 and ascended the ridge on a trail surrounded by groves of whorled loosestrife. Followed a soft grassy ridge with alternating sunny and shady spots—never too hot, never too cool.

Pennsylvania ridge.

Then on down by a stream through tall, cool pines to a clearing—a paradise—full of strawberries and sunshine. We spent about an hour picking strawberries. I ate myself full, then filled my water bottle with berries. We continued up a steep rocky trail through cool woods permeated with the fragrance of laurel to Pulpit Rocks. I took off my pack and stood awestruck on the rocks. In the light of the sun on this clear day, the valley looked like a painting on the canvas of a master. The deep green of the mountainside trees rolled down to the neatly laid-out fields, each separated by a different shade of green or amber. Here and there a tractor unknowingly played the role of the artist's paintbrush, painting stripes into the landscape as it went about its work cutting hay. Metal roofs of barns and farmhouses reflected the sun. To the left was a view of the ridge I'd be walking later, and further on was a faint view of the Delaware Water Gap, about eighty miles away. We sat on these rocks and feasted like never before. Out came the strawberries, rice cakes, honey, milk, and wheat germ, all blended together to make the best strawberry shortcake ever. It's truly a good life!

Strawberry shortcake.

On we went to Pinnacle Rocks and more amazing views and blazing sun, then down the rocky trail to a wide dirt road. We filled the air with songs and chants down past some old farms with bulging corncribs and outhouses to Eckville. Once back into the cool, dark fir forest, a pleasant little stream provided a perfect spot for cooling tired feet. On up an eroded trail to Hawk Mountain and on to Dan's Pulpit—another sunny, rocky overview. Took another break to enjoy the sun, then moved on one and half miles to Dan's Knob lean-to for another strawberry break. Finally at 4, we decided to do some walking and went on eight miles to Don's spring; a 19-mile day. Topped the day off with a bath in the cold spring and meditation in the cool woods.

Up early to a mellow morning broken by lots of real rocky hiking—but just when I got tired of rock hopping the trail became wide and grassy, surrounded by laurel. On up to Bake Oven Knob, and I sat in the sun on the rocky overview. Stopped at Bake Oven lean-to for yet more wild-strawberry shortcake. On over some intense rocky areas, along dirt roads up to a ridge with views of Lehigh River. On through laurel, then the first true sign of summer—the first ripe blueberries. I hiked from one blueberry bush to another for over an hour. The hardest part of the Appalachian Trail for me has been to get past the berry patches. On down rocky descent to Outerbridge shelter with a beautiful spring. Also at the shelter was a newlywed couple. We relinquished the shelter to them as their honeymoon suite, gave them some blueberries, and found a place to camp down the trail. A whip-poor-will began his chant as the full yellow moon rose into the purple sky.

Up at 6—a late start and down over more rocks to the polluted Lehigh River, cars, highways, smells, and sounds. Very quickly we crossed the river and ascended the cliffs on the other side. Both hands and feet were needed to scramble over these rocks. The view from the top was of mountains scored by strip-mining, railroads, and highway. On over the ridge on a hard dirt road open to the sun, reflecting the heat like an oven. This continued to Little Gap, where we figured it was time for a break, so we hitched two miles into a town. I bought a quart of orange sherbet, topped it with fresh blueberries and honey, and feasted on the front porch of the store. Then along came the bread man, who gave us day-old coffee cakes! We hitched back to the trail and struggled on with full bellies over the rocks to Wind Gap, where we met Zeb and camped for the night.

On the trail at 7 and it was already hot. It's been in the nineties for the past two weeks. It was very hazy—a good day for a thunderstorm. On over rocks and through trail overgrown with briars. The view of the Delaware Water Gap was obscured by the fog, so we moved quickly down into the town. At the post office I was met with a lot of pleasant surprises. Many letters, another batch of cookies from Judy, and a care package from home, all filled with love.

I'm getting really close to home. It's only 162 miles to the New York-Connecticut State line. I've now walked 1,185.7 miles and have loved every step of the way, every breath, every day.

SEVEN

In the midst and mist of a summer shower, Jeff and I leave the Delaware Water Gap. The torrent of the weather is complemented by the storm of cars speeding and splashing us as we cross the bridge over the Delaware River from Pennsylvania into New Jersey. Far below us raindrops merge with the surprisingly clean waters of the river. Up into the woods to some familiar sights—a deep ravine cut by a cold clear mountain brook shaded by tall hemlock and rhododendron. Ferns hang from the moss-covered banks, as the water cascades over smooth, polished rocks. Memories of many an afternoon spent in Nettleton's Ravine above my house in Cheshire. Suddenly the South is left behind—the new but familiar world of New England beckons. The fog permeates the dark hemlocks, and shapes fade off into dreams.

Ferns in ravine, Delaware Water Gap.

🌲

Rainy day, turn me inward, hide from me my views of the world in your fog. Let me look into the clouds of my mind. Let your downpour wash the cobwebs from my soul. Let your gentle rain nourish new life to grow in tomorrow's sun . . .

🌲

I sat on a boulder in midstream and watched the mosaic of rocks seemingly dancing on the ripples through the crystal water. On through the hushed softness of the hemlocks. The only voices were the flowing song of the rain and the brook. On up the ridge as the clouds broke to let the sun through. A warm mist rose from the wet plants as the water that fell from the sky like a lion slipped away like a ghost.

As the white clouds raced away and the blue came through, we arrived at Sunfish Pond. The sun sparkled in the pearls of water clinging to the laurel like a necklace of rainbows. I took off my pack and meditated on a rock, and felt the sun's fingers knead deep into my soul. I then plunged into the icy pond and glided into its sparkling depth. We stayed here luxuriating for about three hours, then moved on through the lush laurel to the open, grassy ridgetop blooming with blueberries. I stopped to pick a pint, then went on to meet Jeff on the high point of the ridge with views of tree-covered rolling hills and the beautiful and clean Delaware River. I sat in the warm rays of the evening sun with my book and blueberries and waited for the sun to set. A family out for a summer day's hike passed through our camp at sunset and gave us a bag of dried fruit, coconut, nuts, and candy. After this surprise snack, I set up my tarp and turned in. I kept high and dry in spite of the midnight rainstorm.

Got up at 6 and packed up my wet tarp, donned my poncho and rain cover, and moved out at 6:45. The poncho didn't stay on for long, of course, as it gets like a steam bath inside. On along the grassy ridge with sparse chestnut oak, whorled loosestrife, wild rose, and blueberries everywhere. We descended into a gap blooming with laurel and sweet fern. On down a dirt road tunneled through rhododendron. Frilly grasses and hay-scented fern gave a soft appearance to the rocky ground. A speckled fawn and later a doe bounded off with tail flags flying.

As I sit on a rock on Rattlesnake Mountain, I reach down for a snack of the plumpest blueberries yet. I've grown quite attached to these blueberries along the trail, which now surround us. I feel like a parent watching a child grow, as they go from bare branches to buds, flowers to fruit. Two and a half months I've watched. Slowly, silently, I've grown with them, and together we offer the fruit of our souls to the universe.

On along the rocky ridge with rattlesnake fern above my head and laurel blossoms hanging into the trail under my nose. The view of the ridge was surprising for New Jersey. Forest-covered hills as far as I could see. This whole ridge—from the Delaware Water Gap to High Point in New Jersey—is called Kittatinny Mountain. Kittatinny means "greatest hill" for the Lenni-Lenape Indians. Staying at Brink Road lean-to tonight. The shelter was full of crane flies, so I set my tarp outside. I had droves of mosquitoes to deal with, so I also set up my mosquito netting. Was sung to sleep by the music of mosquitoes. I was visited by a skunk looking for a snack in my pack, but he left without an argument.

Under cloudy skies and air full of mosquitoes, we set out in the morning over a rocky trail and descended to Route 206 and a bakery. After a breakfast of carrot bread, I went on alone as Jeff hitched on to Unionville to get to the post office before it closed. I moved on through aspen trees on a soft pine-needled path. The sprawling arms of a chestnut oak reached out over the dense, diverse green undergrowth lighted by pink and white laurel, bush honeysuckle, and yellow loosestrife. A towhee scolded me for intruding on his blueberry patch. On over a rocky trail, over cloudy Sunrise Mountain into Highpoint State Park, down by a mucky marsh shrouded by mystical mist wrapped around gray dead trees. The silence was broken by the shrill of a pileated woodpecker.

Just as raindrops began to break the surface of Lake Marcia, the highest body of water in New Jersey, I reached High Point, the highest mountain in New Jersey. No view, of course. On down to New Salem Road—a country lane through hay fields and rundown farms. Luckily, the road was cooled by the rain. After about four miles, I caught up with old John Collins again. He was looking like a Swiss yodeler with shorts and a cap. I also reunited with Jeff in Unionville, where John bought me a spaghetti dinner, which was welcome after the day's 25-mile walk. John had gotten ahead by skipping Virginia. We had a pleasant reunion, then all slept in the cemetery.

John left early in the morning as Jeff and I meditated; then we did some grocery shopping in town. I've been spending between five and ten dollars per week for groceries, which includes food sent from the Emporium. We left town at about 9:30 and proceeded down the A.T. highway—roads and more roads. We met John walking in the wrong direction—lost—following his compass and trying his best to be a woodsman. I pointed him in the right direction, and we all went on together. By now the thunder was rumbling over the cornfields, and the rain had started falling. We continued on roads to Liberty Corners and searched for trail blazes in an overgrown hay field. All the trees were hidden beneath a cloak of poison ivy and Virginia creeper that covered the blazes. We split up and followed various possible roads through the wet hay until Jeff found a blaze. Back on the trail. A hard rain was falling as we climbed Pochuck Mountain on a narrow trail with overhanging bushes—it was like going through a car wash.

Brushing past the glistening wet leaves, we moved on to more paved roads through farms, then right through a development. Hiked on through suburbs. Stopped at a pond in the midst of the housing development for a snack of blueberries and to rest our wet feet. We wrung out our socks and sloshed on through Vernon Valley to Route 94, about nine miles of road walking. Here we parted with John—he went to visit his sister in New York. Jeff and I went on about one half mile to the base of Wawayanda Mountain and made camp. As the rain began, I set up my tarp and listened to the raindrop rhapsody. The music was interrupted by the buzz of mosquitoes. The rain must have driven every mosquito in the woods to the shelter of my tarp. I put up a mosquito netting, as Jeff squirmed, swore, and swatted. We were like two flies in a spiderweb.

Finally dawn broke, and we wasted no time getting up and moving in spite of the rain. On up the Wawayanda Mountain and over slippery rocks along an overflowing brook. After one hour of slipping and sloshing, we reached the top for a view of rain and clouds. We dripped on along the ridge—boots getting wetter and heavier all the time. On through mud up to the ankles. A dirt road came as a welcome relief from the wet brush and muddy trail. On down the dirt road past Cascade Lake through another development up to Passport Rock under a cloak of fog offering only scant views of Greenwood Lake. Had a fun climb over Cat Rock, named for the bobcats that once lived there, and the Pinnacles, then down to another road and Whispering Pines campground. The guy there let us take a quick hot shower before his boss came back.

On into Harriman State Park through a hemlock forest to a pond full of purple flowers, on through the "lemon squeezer"—huge boulders with a narrow path between them. We camped upon the flat grassy ridge. A cool breeze came up to sweep the storm away. Yellow and red mushrooms were scattered here and there in the wet forest debris. Finally, after such a miserable day, the rain stopped and the sky cleared. It was a beautiful evening. I went for a little walk along the ridge with soft, lush grass between the oaks and hickory. The late-afternoon sun turned patches from yellow to amber, green to gold. The soft seed tassels waved like a dreamy mist in the light breeze. I sat on a rock just absorbing it all—such contrast to a day so harsh—now so mellow. Birds again sang their evening songs, and again we ended our day in the colors of the sun.

Jeff at Harriman State Park, New York.

Just as the day ended in colors, in colors the new morning began. The gentle dawn breeze caused a new day to stir me from my sleep but not from my dreaming. The morning mist lingered and merged with the soft frail cloud of tall grasses. On over the grassy ridge as the breeze spoke of loving in hushed tones through the hemlock trees. Walking soft on a cushion of pine needles. The darkness of the pines broken by dancing sunlight sparkling on the emerald mosses.

I walk silently and slowly in hopes of seeing deer. The picture in my mind becomes reality as I sight a doe, barely visible against a background of fallen trees and pine needles. The darkness of hemlock is contrasted by the sunlit beech and birch glimmering in yellow and green.

I ascended a hill on a ladder of roots with white laurel in the sun as pure as the air and the day. Moved on down to the Lake Tiorati Park—part of Bear Mountain Park. The swimming area and snack bar were closed, so we moved on up Goshen and Letterrock Mountains through sparse oaks and grassy slopes to Letterrock lean-to. Up a steep, rocky climb and across giant rock slabs. We sat in the sun on cliffs enveloped by mountains with views of the Hudson River. We descended and crossed the Palisades Parkway. With all this beauty, I can't believe we're only a half hour away from New York City. A perfect day to climb the sheer cliffs of Bear Mountain. We struggled our way to the top only to find droves of tourists in cars and a stone lookout tower. But that was just the beginning—on down we went to the sound of carnival music coming from the skating rink in Bear Mountain Park. Along with the rink was a lodge, a museum, a pool, a pond, and an amusement park, all designed so the city folk can get a little taste of "nature."

Being slightly averse to crowds, we passed through quickly across the Bear Mountain Bridge over the Hudson River. This is the low point of the trail—115 feet. On up the steep ascent of Canada Hill, a rough climb after a long day. We planned to camp here but moved on through farms, hay fields, and horses to Route 9. We hitched to a restaurant for a salad and baked potato, then walked back in the darkness to the trail. I just rolled out my sleeping bag and a ground cloth and watched the stars. I've felt the grandeur of the mountaintops and humility under the stars.

The next morning, on through cool, pleasant maple, birch, and oak woods. Following crumbling, tumbling, stone walls that remain as a monument to farmers of decades past who over-cleared these woods and plucked these rocks from their fields. Occasionally a large oak or sugar maple spared by those farmers stood amongst the second growth of trees.

This brings me out to Route 84 in New York State—a convenient place to hitch home for a Fourth of July break and to install a pool at my parents' home. I'll get back on the trail here in about a week to continue on the last seven hundred miles to Maine.

In the past two and a half months and 1,300 miles, I've seen the cradle of spring gilded with golden sun, full of buds and birds, I've been rocked by the wind and lullabied by the sweet song of Mother Earth, whose breath is the breath of life, inhaling the crystalline spark of spring sun. I've seen this spark move through every tree and ignite flames of life from within them. The spark touched the heart of the earth, and it burst open with a flurry of flowers. I've heard the song of mountain brooks dancing over rocks filled with tears of joy flowing freely from the heart of Mother Nature filling the veins of the reincarnated season. I've heard the song of love sung by a thousand birds building their own cradle to harbor their new creations.

Every nest is filled with eggs, and seeds burst forth into flower to brighten and lighten the path. With every rising and setting of the sun, the days get longer and the flowers fuller. Broken eggs are scattered along the trail, and new eyes look upon the world. The spring flowers ripen to summer fruit, and another step is climbed on the path toward eternity. So many sights and smells impossible to describe—never to be forgotten—forever implanted in my soul lie the glimpsing memories of a dream.

EIGHT

A fter walking for miles on paved roads through several New York towns, I finally entered a hay field and with a sigh of relief I drew a breath, taking in the sweet smell of fresh-cut hay. Farm equipment lay resting after a hard day's work. On through the woods and onto a dirt road with a roadside garden of black-eyed Susans, Queen Anne's lace, daisy flea-bane, horsemint, oxeye daisies, water willow, cottonwood, and sumac. Horses grazed in pastures with a backdrop of mountains. Poke—no longer the soft, tender edible delights of springtime—now stood tall and elegant like Oriental ornamental trees with hanging clusters of purple green berries. Onto a paved road with stone walls on each side separating families of hemlocks. Tall gray birch contrasted with the dark hemlocks. Water willows and alder indicated that I was entering swampland. Droves of mosquitoes confirmed it. Came across a little weathered shed surrounded by gray birch, poplar, and a tangle of blackberry brambles and made this "slanty shanty" my home for the night.

Lots of birdsongs, but their melodies are interrupted by the drone of airplanes and the whistle of trains. I feel like I'm living on the edge of two worlds now, feeling the magnetism of each drawing on my soul. The rush I get from my life of humanity and the peace of my solitude in the world of eternity. Balancing on the "threshold of a dream" as Thoreau said, "It's not that I love humanity the less, but that I love nature the more."

I'm using my new air mattress for the first time tonight. I bought it not only for sleeping but also in anticipation of the lakes and rivers of New England. It will be handy for fording streams and for floating in the sun on the many lakes I'll be encountering.

After setting up my camp, I sit and watch as the evening breeze brings a curtain of darkness around me. The stage is set—all props take their places.

Fireflies—evening eyes
Moonbeam through the trees
Aspen leaves
On evening breeze
Pleasant memories

A fox, out stalking its next meal, yipped in the marsh below as I drifted off to sleep. Up at 5:30 and into my morning routine of exercises and meditation, then a breakfast of wheat germ and soy-granule mixture with honey, raisins, and milk.

Out into the birdsongs and a bath in the wet overgrown fields. A restless wren darted about in a cherry tree. Blackberries galore. On through an overgrown apple orchard full of deer tracks as deerflies circle my head. On into the village of Wabatuck, New York, with its old-fashioned craft village and across the Ten Mile River. Took a bath in a deep brook and watched iridescent damselflies and green dragonflies dart and hover about. Japanese beetles made skeletons of the greenery. Crossed the New York-Connecticut border at the crest of Schaghticoke Mountain and signed the register. On over the rugged Indian Rocks with views of the Housatonic River and into Rattlesnake Ravine, a small ravine reported to be full of snakes. Up Mt. Algo through hemlock, then through woods of maple and oak scattered with Christmas tree fern, Indian pipes, and mushrooms. On down a very steep, treacherous descent to Route 341 and the Kent School Farm. The trail then went steeply up Kent Rocks, completely painted over by lovers and Kent School students. "Fools' names and fools' faces always appear in public places."

Road walking, Webatuck, New York.

On over the ridge of Macedonia Mountain with blueberries and black-berries side by side, then down through birch and hemlock to Macedonia Brook Road. I re-entered the woods filled with old stone walls, up Chase Mountain. I felt like I was walking with the spirits of the old-time farmers in Robert Frost's poem "Mending Walls." I picked a spot for the night near Chase Mountain lean-to next to a brook, then set up my tarp and mosquito netting in a little clearing surrounded by maidenhair fern. I was sung to sleep by my "dream stream." A perfect night's sleep—cool air—few bugs.

I liked it so much I didn't get up till 6. Washed up and meditated as the sun rose over the mountain and shone golden green through the trees and climbed and shined on the lacework of webs. A mixture of oaks, ash, hickory, maple, and yellow birch made my roof. As I sat on a rock talking to my stream, a chipmunk played hide-and-seek in the rocks, and a flycatcher swooped down over the stream and snatched a snack. On down the trail flowing with runoff, then up the steep, rocky climb to South Cobble Mountain, which offered very rewarding views of green mountains and mist-filled valleys. On along the open ridge of Cobble Mountain filled with blueberries and excellent views of the Catskills and the Taconics. Flushed out a family of grouse as I walked along on this very hot, humid day.

On down another steep, wet, rocky descent using my hands, feet, staff, trees, and anything else I could grab to prevent a Nantucket sleigh ride down the mountain. Down into Meadow camp and picnic area, where I washed my hair in Macedonia Brook. On into a wildlife sanctuary on a wet trail through tall interrupted fern and orange mushrooms, blue beech and crisscrossing streams. Up Caleb's Peak, with a rock cliff overlooking the Housatonic Valley.

Summit of Indian Rocks, Connecticut.

A hawk soared on the breeze over farms nestled in the tree-covered hills. On down more mountain goat trails over St. Johns Ledges, then down on dirt roads to the Housatonic River. Entered a grove of tall red pines. The sun shone pink on the columns, and the wind spoke in the towering branches. I cooled off in one of the many streams flowing into the Housatonic.

The trail continued along the river, then I crossed on Cornwall Bridge. I stopped at the general store for ice cream, cantaloupe, peaches, and orange juice. On steeply up Dark Entry Road. After walking all day along the river, listening to its constant flow, I now stopped to dwell on the silence of the hemlock forest.

Here I meet Rachel driving the "support van" for Warren Doyle and his U Conn Trail Trotters. Warren holds the record for doing the trail the fastest and seeing the least. Two years ago he "hiked" it all in 60 and one-half days. His group is now doing from 20 to 30 miles a day, and some do as much as 40 miles a day. Most carry very light packs, and some carry nothing, as their support van meets them each night with their food and sleeping gear. Their scratched and scraped legs tell tales of many hours of night hiking. This is another record for Warren—the largest group to do the trail—as he terms it "the longest volunteer march in history." The record holder—out to "conquer" nature—seeking glorification of the ego. It would be a much more difficult task to conquer the ego and glorify nature.

If I wanted to march I'd join the army; if I wanted to run I'd join a track team. I don't think the founders of the trail intended it for marching, jogging, or stumbling in the darkness. I see it as an opportunity to get away from the fast pace of society, to slow down—to reunite with the flow of the universe. To forget where I'm going—to be here now.

I moved on about a mile to Dark Entry Stream and got up my tarp on a rise between the stream and an old well-worn dirt road in a forest of hemlock intermingled with black birch. This was Coltsfoot Mountain. Many stone remnants of the old farms hold the mystery of the past. It was fun to speculate on which one was a barn, which a house, where the well was, etc., going back in time with these stony skeletons.

Up at 5 A.M. and went on upstream past cascades and an old stone dam. It was 80 degrees at 7:30. Wound around, up and down through hemlocks over rocky ridges and steep, rocky descents to a road through farms and field. On into the holy hush of cathedral pines—soft path, soft light. Out onto more roads—stopped and lay back in a brook and just let it flow over me. Striped maple with green clusters of seeds hung like mobiles over the muddy trail. On through pines into a small field. I stood in the middle in the sun and breeze. On one side, dark pines—on the other, tall, straight poplar quivering in the heightening breeze.

Met a group from the Cheshire Reformatory, and we all stayed in Dean Ravine. I sat until dark on a rock by the stream. Little fish tried to nibble on my toes, and a shy crayfish peered out from under a rock. The nature of life unfolds in the flowing and singing of a stream. Poured rain all night, but I stayed high and dry on my air mattress and didn't float away.

Slipped and stumbled over wet rocks and roots the next morning. Down the ravine past cascades and falls, then through hemlock forest carpeted by club mosses. Under cloudy, threatening skies, I proceeded up Barrack Mountain. A difficult climb and descent worsened by rain. On down to a road lined with bouncing Bet and black-eyed Susans to a café outside Falls Village. The light rain cooled the roads as I proceeded through Falls Village across the Housatonic River. On up to Limestone Spring through tall hemlocks that seem to hold up the sky. The rain turned to mist as it filtered through the hemlock needles.

On through the rain over Bear Mountain, the high point of Connecticut, 2,316 feet. The sun began playing hide-and-seek with the clouds as I descended Bear Mountain. Red bunchberry brightened the ground cover as I crossed the Massachusetts-Connecticut line. The air got cooler as I descended into Sages Ravine. Down the fern-covered rocky slopes, and I found a good spot along the brook to set up camp and dry out. I took a bath in the brook and meditated.

All alone in the Sages Ravine, I feel like a prince in his great hall decked with green lace and silk. I feel like a sage, and this is my ravine—my temple. But most of all I feel like a child— this is my playground, where my mind is free to expand and fill this great hollow, and I can be anything I desire.

Spent a beautiful crisp night cuddled in my down bag. Woke up to blue sky and chirping birds. The air seemed washed clean and cool as the brook. Lacy fern banners waved in the morning breeze. The beauty of the falls and pools was astounding.

As I walk through the ravine I think, I wouldn't miss a day like this for the world. But the world is already mine—as far as my eyes can see and as far as my feet can walk.

I can't describe the beauty of this day. It must be perceived to be believed. The words that tell of the wonders of this world are sung by the wind in the leaves and the chimes of a robin.

I feel like an honored guest as I reach the open peak of Mt. Everett. Swallows dart busily about, and my arrival is heralded by thrushes and mockingbirds. The best blueberries are laid out for a feast, and the sun illuminates the scenery. I sit on the mountaintop eating blueberries and watch the puffy clouds float by.

On through scrub oaks and dwarf pines over Mt. Undine. Dragonflies and Carolina locusts buzzed about the open sunny ridgetop. My faithful friend, the towhee, has been with me since Georgia. Down very steeply to Jug End Road shaded by sugar maples. A goldfinch wove a yellow path across the deep blue sky. A phoebe darted and dipped after bugs around a pond. A cardinal streaked across the road like a flaming arrow. On across a valley on dirt roads and up East and Warner Mountains past Butternut Basin ski area. Entered Beartown State Park and camped on Benedict Pond under huge gray birch trees.

Through white clouds of gray birch floating above a sea of hay-scented fern, I sail, then fly on the surrealistic yellow-green sunlight dancing through beech leaves. I glide weightless—dream-walking on a soft carpet of needles into the dim pinks and reds of a spruce forest. All is silent except the chanting of the breeze through the branches. I feel like I'm stepping into Maxwell Parrish's "Dreamlight." I round a bend and there in the trail are two walking pine boughs, a mama and baby porcupine.

Sunset from Mt. Greylock, the highest point in Massachusetts.

On down dirt roads past some incredible estates into Tyringham. Up to Becket Mountain through a patch of tart red raspberries and down to Finerly Pond. Took a swim and feasted on rice cakes and fratina. After dark I heard some splashing and crashing behind me. I sat on a rock and watched a beaver sliding about in the murky pond, occasionally beating his flat tail on the water. On through the towns of Dalton and Cheshire on a windy, gray day. As the sky cleared I ascended steeply toward Jones Nose.

I stopped to sample some juneberries and was stunned by stands of fuchsia fireweed. Up through meadows in the full summer splendor of fireweed, goldenrod, yarrow, and steeplebush. The wind made waves of colors in the sunny field. Views of Otis Ridge ski area appeared across distant slopes.

Ascending Mt. Greylock, Massachusetts's high point, I come upon a group from a camp for the deaf. Though unable to hear the songs of the birds and the wind, they experience the world with their other senses, which tell the story on their inner voice.

Now I sit watching the sunset on Mt. Greylock, and feel the energy on the Berkshires breeze. Tomorrow I'll view the sunset in Vermont.

NINE

J ust as I was ready to leave, up walked David from Nova Scotia, and Cornwall from Cornwall—a stray dog that followed David from Cornwall Bridge, Connecticut. We walked together down Greylock and up through oaks and birch to a bare ridgetop full of blueberries and sunshine. I bathed my body with sunshine and filled it up with blueberries, then moved on to the Vermont border. There at the state line is the southern terminus of the Long Trail, which proceeds 260 miles due north through Vermont to the Canadian border. The Appalachian Trail and the Long Trail are one for 100 miles to Sherburne Pass, just north of Killington, Vermont. The Appalachian Trail then heads east toward New Hampshire.

On through woods of yellow and gray birch feathered with ferns and carpeted with club mosses.

On along the beautifully maintained Long Trail. The brush has been cut back, and "stepping stone" logs were placed for crossing muddy creeks. Staying in Seth Warner lean-to. This was the first shelter I've slept in since the Shenandoah. Strolled down to the stream that flowed over moss-softened rocks through hemlock-darkened woods. Took a bath and meditated on a cool, mossy mat. Ate, read, and went to bed.

Pillars of light, gray birch in Vermont.

Vermont . . . such a magical spell it casts upon you.
Vermont . . . older than your weathered barns
and wrinkled faces.
I seek your birch wood charms and your hidden places.
Vermont . . . you wizard so old.
Your secrets are heard but cannot be told.

I was awakened at 5 by a wood peewee. I meditated in a grove of gray birch, and my mind flowed through these pillars of purity reaching up to the temple of the sun. Up and out past a peat bog. In the bog were some pitcher plants. I found the larvae of a mosquito that breeds only in pitcher plant water. Soon I found more mosquitoes than I wanted, so I moved on. A hungry hairy woodpecker hammered a hemlock. Bluebead clintonia lined the path. I leaped from bog to bog across a marsh. Then onto dry land and into a spruce forest. Here lay two skeletons of an old homestead not tough enough for Vermont. The living forest cleanses its wounds slowly with new life—only time will hide the scar.

I stopped at a brook to wash out my socks and have lunch. David and Cornwall caught up, and we went on to Congdon Camp shelter. Shelters on the Long Trail are little cabins with doors and windows. We signed the register and moved on through a field of ferns bordered by Vermont's famous sugar maples. We feasted on juneberries, then went up into an upland meadow studded with steeplebush and gilded with goldenrod. This was Harmond Hill, which overlooked Bennington and the Bennington Monument. On down to Route 9, then the long ascent of Glastonbury Mountain. The woods progressed from beech to birch to spruce at the top.

Finally, we got to the Glastonbury Mountain lean-to. I cooked an omelet for dinner and traded half with David for some chocolate pudding. After dinner we went up to a fire tower and climbed the crow's nest above a sea of blue spruce and watched the sunset over the waves of mountains. When we got back we found that Cornwall had tried to make friends with a porcupine and ended up looking like a pincushion. We spent half the night plucking quills from his snout. All night the porcupine chattered outside the lean-to, seemingly laughing at Cornwall. The shelter was freshly creosoted to keep the porcupine from eating it.

On down through smells of spruce, the forest floor blanketed with emerald green masses studded with wood sorrel. On over Big Rock, 3,290 feet, and down to Stratton Pond. Here we met the area caretaker and got a fire permit for the section. These caretakers are hired by the Green Mountain Club to manage this heavily used area. The cool water at the pond came as a welcome relief from the 90-degree heat. Ate a lunch of rice cakes, peanut butter, and honey, then moved on past Bourne Pond to Sweeney lean-to. Here we met some more people hired by the Green Mountain Club working on a trail reroute.

The next morning I was out early and walked six miles to the town of Manchester Center. Picked up some much needed food and some much appreciated mail at the post office, then hitched back to the trail. As I was leaving town, I met up with David and Cornwall, and we began the ascent of Bromley Mountain with full packs. The air temperature was 105 degrees. When I left town, sweat poured off my body. Finally, a brook—I just lay back with my feet up on a rock and let it flow over me. On up steeply through the woods and onto a ski trail to the summit. Here we met a bunch of people staying in the skiers' warming hut at the mountaintop. They were going to a bluegrass/folk music festival at the bottom of the mountain the next day. Dave and I decided to stay also.

Brought my pack up the observation tower and meditated in the sunset over those magnificent mountains. I stepped up top, watching the stars appear and move across the sky. I marked their progress by the position of the Big Dipper and watched the world turn. Shooting stars glowed in their moment's glory, and then merged with the darkness.

Revelations flash . . . Like shooting stars they come.
Eternal truth burns like the endless sun . . .

I woke in the blue before dawn and watched all the stars fall into the rising sun. Heard some good old Appalachian country music and ate corn on the cob at the music festival. Square-danced with the local folks and had a fine time. Spent another night in the tower on Bromley, then descended the next morning past some whorled asters and blackberry brambles into Mad Tom Ravine.

Another hot day as I sweat up Styles Peak and Peru Peak. It's at least 100 degrees, and the climbing's rough. Hot sun, stab deep into my body with your pitchforks of purity. Let sweat stream from the springs of my soul. Whip away the whirlwinds of worldliness—make me whole. Melt away the mountains of madness. Let me climb to the temple of light. Fill my heart with love and gladness. Cleanse me in the pools of life . . .

The echoes of my footsteps and the splashing rains on the roads leading toward Hanover, New Hampshire, awaken me from my Vermont visions. I stand on the bridge over the Connecticut River and look back through a misty curtain of rain and tears. Through the haze, I see a rainbow arching back 1,700 miles, radiating from the eye of a dream. Each day a new color is mixed and added as I walk on the rays of light toward the rainbow's end.

I lean over the rail of the bridge. Below, raindrops make circles, which merge with each other and then melt into the current. I exchange greetings with two men in a canoe. They drift on toward the ocean, I drift toward the sky. Paths

crossing, going in different directions, but all journeys end
in the same spot, deep in the heart of the wanderer.

On into Hanover and down the blue-blazed sidewalk side trail to the Dartmouth Outing Club headquarters. I signed the register and found a friendly fraternity house in which to spend the night. Cornwall met me on the steps of the frat house, and inside were David and the entire U Conn group. I wondered if the storm inside would be worse than the one outside. I managed to find a quiet corner for my stuff, took a shower, and meditated. Later, over twenty Thru-Hikers converged on Thayer Dining Hall for an all-you-can-eat dinner.

Spirits ran high among the hikers, and the discussion turned to anticipation of Mt. Katahdin and speculations on when the end will come. My path is not bounded by time, but stretches on with each rising of the sun. My path has no end, but turns with the changes of the seasons, forming a circle encompassing the universe, with its center deep in my soul.

I hit Thayer Hall again for breakfast, then headed down the roads out of town. Back to the woods. Bright yellow mushrooms glowed like the moon on a sea of green mosses. Nuthatches did acrobatics on pine trees. I came to an open summit, and a purple finch bounced about on a blue green mat of reindeer lichen. Chickadees busily reaped the harvest of late summer seeds. Out onto a road past farms and meadows. Cowbells chimed melancholy notes into the blue afternoon sky. Back to the woods, where I cooled my feet in a trickling brook.

. . . My brook and I, gently, softly we flow through hidden corners of our world; we go pouring ourselves into every shape we give, filling all, becoming all we live.

We sing, we dance, outside the mainstream; with laughter and tears we follow our dream

Until in the ocean all brooks meet as one and discover eternity in the light of the sun . . .

I lay back on a bed of pine needles and looked up at the blue sky filling the spaces between the green branches. A nuthatch looked at me upside down, and red squirrels gathered pinecones in their treetop world. Here in these woods we find all that we need. As the afternoon drifted on, toward darkness, I drifted on to dreams. These pines became my shelter for the night.

I awoke to the singing of birds and chattering of squirrels and meditated as images of the first rays of the morning sun danced through my head. As I walked along, church bells in the valley told me that it was Sunday.

> . . . Church bells in the valley ring,
> Remind me of the day
> Voices united together sing,
> In one voice they pray
> Out here the many songs of
> God are sung
> By the birds, the flowers, the wind and sun . . .

The sprawling arms of an old sugar maple seemed to be supporting the sky. On through a forest of beech and maple into a valley of small farms. Walked down a lane between fences. The smells of fresh-cut hay and the baying of sheep and cattle filled the air. On up into a red-pine grove and took a bath in a brook. Then through overgrown pastures full of flowers bordered by sugar maples. The grade became steep up to Holt's Ledges—sheer cliffs affording an overlook of valleys, mountains, and a lake in the distance. On down to Trapper John's lean-to for the night. I meditated by the brook, then cooked fratina for supper over a fire. As the sun went down, an owl began his hunting and hooting.

Morning brought the sunrise and another summer day. Summertime burrs clung to my socks, my pack stuck to my back. Flowers were turning to seed, the ferns were sporing—next year's life compacted in this year's seeds. Autumn's paintbrush already streaked yellow on the leaves of bell-wort. Vireos and peewees called in the trees, and toads were the most abundant animals. I sampled Indian cucumber root and hog peanuts. Heal-all, Indian tobacco, and a variety of mints flavored the air, and pitchforks of running pine grew everywhere. Ferns of many kinds also grew abundantly in these moist woods. Sensitive, bracken, hay-scented, New York, maidenhair, rattlesnake, interrupted, royal cinnamon, Christmas, and rock polypody, all in a ten-foot circle around me.

The clouds began building for a thunderstorm; pace quickened. The spirits were with me, and I arrived at Cube Mountain shelter and got cleaned up just as the rain started. I felt like I was sitting in a manger watching life being created as the thunder and lightning crashed. The storm passed, and before me unfolded a paradise of saintly birch and dark spruce.

Up to the rain-washed morning, with the sun gleaming on wet leaves.

Wind-driven sun showers cooled me as I climbed Cube Mountain. Up the bare quartz rock mountaintop, the rock warmed by the sun, I watched the clouds in the valley disappear on the breeze. Ate blueberries and watched a hawk circle the summit. A skull-and-crossbones sign warned of a steep descent—no switchback, making a rough, eroded steep trail. Conditions would be greatly improved if switchbacks were used to prevent the inevitable erosion of such overused trails. These trails, up to the beginning of the White Mountain National Forest, are maintained by the Dartmouth

Outing Club. On down a road to Lake Armington, where I met two girls with a key to the Dartmouth Outing Club cabin on the lake. They invited me to stay, and I got a shower at the Walt Whitman Camp next door. I took a moonlight canoe ride and gave thanks for the simple pleasures of my life—to be simply aware of the simple things of life. I sailed on moonbeams across the lake and watched the stars appear.

On the next morning, after an early dip in the lake, through the little town of Glecliff, then the climbing began. Mt. Mossilauke, 4,810 feet, loomed ahead. The climb up Mossilauke was quite pleasant— spruce and streams—but the view was obscured by clouds, and the descent was treacherous. Ladders were installed in the rocks to aid in the steep descent. This was only an introduction to the Whites. On down to Kinsman Notch and up steeply. Decided to call it a day by some water. Set up my tarp, meditated, ate a fast dinner, and had no trouble getting to sleep.

Woke to a heavily overcast day and moved on over the Kinsman Ridge, without a view. Over South Kinsman (4,363 feet) and North Kinsman (4,274 feet). Down steeply and on past the first Appalachian Mountain Club hut at Lonesome Lake. The trail through the Whites is maintained by the A.M.C., and the hut system is provided for lodging and meals—for a price. I stopped in at Lonesome Lake for some hot cocoa and moved on to a brook on the Kinsman Pond side trail, where I spent the night.

The sky began to clear, and the trees whirled in the wind. On down to Whitehorse Bridge in Franconcia Notch and up steadily through fir and an amazing variety of mosses. On up Little Haystack Mountain and above the tree line. The trail became narrow and rocky, and the wind nearly swept me away. Chartreuse lichens decorated the rocks. The excitement rose as I climbed over the open ridge. The wind was strong, but the sun was warm—a perfect day. On up to Mt. Lincoln, 5,109 feet. Sat there on the summit open to the full force of the wind and the sun, and felt the energy of the White Mountains swirl around me. Quite a few people came up via side trails from Greenleaf Hut, about one mile down. A cloud of smoke from Mt. Washington's Cog Railway was visible. From here on I referred to it as the "Smog Railway."

On down some rough climbs over the north peak of Lafayette to the Garfield Ridge and the summit of Mt. Garfield, 4,488 feet. I meditated facing into the wind and soared like an eagle in the golden sunset sky above the glowing mountains. The evening profiles of the mountains disappeared into the night, and I sought the warmth of my down sleeping bag to watch the star show. As the stars swept across the sky, I was swept into a dream and awakened in the silence of the rising sun.

On through fir and birch—their roots tangled and twisted over rocks to find a foothold among the cracks. Goldenrod and bunchberry contrasted with the green mosses. On to Galehead hut for cocoa and biscuits, then up the steep, rocky climb to South Twin Summit, 4,926 feet. Mountain sandwort and diapensia grow among the rocks in this alpine environment. Mountain cranberry formed mats studded with red berries. On down the Twinway Ridge to Mt. Guyot campground, one mile off the trail. This was the only spot with water within five miles, so I paid a dollar to the A.M.C. caretaker to stay there.

Left early under cloudy, windy, threatening skies. On through twisted, dwarfed, gnarled fir along Zealand Ridge. Feasted on blueberries. Down through peeling birch and over rocky trails to Zealand Hut. Played in the brook and waterfalls for about two hours, then descended to Crawford Notch.

Evening fell as I ascended from Crawford Notch through tall beech trees into pines. As the sun lowered, a pink cast rose amidst the pines. Red squirrels darted under logs, but their daytime chatter had ceased. No sound except the wind.

I sat on the open face of Webster Cliffs. The sun fell below the mountains across the notch and added shades of pastels to the sky and mountains. The wind sent a chill to my bones, and I sought the shelter of the trees. The trees were dwarfed and bare on the windward side. I set up my tarp to block the wind and sought the warmth and comfort of my sleeping bag.

Woke up. Meditated and had breakfast without leaving my sleeping bag. Out at 6:30 and moved fast to keep warm. Over Mt. Jackson, 4,052 feet, and stopped at Mispah Springs hut to warm up. Out again into the cloudy cold, windy, wild day. Rode the wind above the tree line of Mt. Clinton, 4,310 feet, and took the side trail up Mt. Eisenhower, 4,761 feet. In the Presidential Range, the Appalachian Trail passes the summits and has side-loop trails to each summit. Despite the clouds and wind, I took each summit loop. The wind literally blew me up Mt. Franklin, 5,004 feet. My pack acted like a sail; several times I was knocked against the rocks by the gusts.

Franconia Ridge, Presidential Range, New Hampshire.

This above-tree-line zone appears barren, lifeless—a world of sterile rock scoured of the spark of life by the relentless wind. A zone rising from the earth toward the moon—but of neither—a world of its own. A zone too harsh for the carefree in life. These mountains are home for the unique and hardy few who humble themselves to this hellish heaven on earth.

Humbled, dwarfed, clothed in a waxy sheath, and seeking shelter from the storm among the rocks, diapensia, mountain sandwort, and mountain cranberry thrive. These seemingly lifeless rocks become the harbors for life—behind each, out of the wind, is a garden of alpine flora, alpine willow herb, alpine speedwell, mountain a vens, alpine goldenrod, one-flowered wintergreen. The very faces of the rocks lie hidden, camouflaged, encrusted by chartreuse, blue, green, and black lichens.

I rounded Mt. Monroe and below me was the Lakes at the Clouds hut.

The two small spring-fed lakes danced with waves in the wake of the wind.

Mt. Washington loomed in a halo of clouds.

I went down to the hut and huddled inside over hot cocoa with Tom, Harry, George and Dan, and some other Thru-Hikers not seen for many miles. The sun finally reached the summit of Mt. Washington. I left my pack in the hut, donned my poncho to break the wind, and took a jaunt to the top of New England. The winds at the weather station read 50 knots, and the temperature plus-three degrees. I had to brace myself against the rocks to take pictures. It was not the wind but the storm of tourists who drove their cars or rode the Smog Railway up the mountain that drove me away.

A cold climb up Mt. Washington, New Hampshire.

These people see the view, they feel the wind, but it only drives them shivering within the walls of the lodge or back to their cars. Do they become aware of the real power of the mountain or are they only aware of their ability to hide from the elements within man-made comforts? They reach the summit, but have they felt the living heart of the mountain, have they caressed its body with their feet? Have they sweated like lovers struggling together to reach the sky? Have the breath of their souls and the breath of the wind become one? And when upon the

summit, does the vision carry them on—souls united—soar-
ing to the sun? What do they learn of love and mountains?

I returned to the hut but found it crawling with tourists. Joined by Dan, we escaped the howling of kids into the howling wind. We returned, and Dan's hike staff was nowhere in sight. The friend, the companion, with him since Springer Mt., Georgia, night and day, rain and shine, had now become a souvenir for some insensitive tourist.

To the top of Mt. Monroe. I sat down in between the rocks and meditated as the afternoon sun shined through the prism of clouds on the horizon, sending colors dancing on the mountaintops. The sky and the mountains now glowed with gold. It was difficult to tell if the mountains were radiating their own glow or reflecting the sun. Regardless, they became one in color and then faded, losing their identity in the oneness of night.

Back at the hut, I find an empty bunk and hide from the tur-
moil of tourists. The hut is silent as I slip out into the mysti-
cal morning mists. Into the cold clouds I am swept. I climb
invisible mountains on a stairway of rocks leading to heaven.
No views of distant lands—only my own reflection in the fog.
Each step leads me deeper into the void. Each step leads me to
feel—my mind meanders in the mists. I linger on the clouds
between heaven and earth—I feel my connection to both.

I followed the Cairns across the Cog Railway tracks to a sign directing me to the summit of Mt. Clay, 5,532 feet. My breath merged with the fog and disappeared on the wind. Huge monoliths appeared, and then disappeared in the fog. I faced the full rage of the tempest on Mt. Jefferson, 5,715 feet. Over Mt. Adams, 5,798 feet, and on to Madison Hut for lunch. The clouds scattered on the wind, and the summit of Mt. Madison appeared. I climbed its garnet-filled rocks and raised my arms in praise of the sun. Mt. Washington, the Wildcat Range, and the Presidential Range now were visible. Again back to the soft green world below tree line. Back to the murmur of brooks and soft hemlock needles underfoot.

I moved fast past the people at Pinkham Notch and up Wildcat Mountain in the steepest, roughest climb yet on the trail. I camped halfway up by a spring. The morning sun glowed pink on Mt. Washington on the opposite ridge. The day began with more steep ascents to the Wildcat Lift Line lodge. I watched a red-tailed hawk through a view machine. On down what the guidebook described as a precipitous descent into Carter Notch, up Carter Dome, 4,843 feet, over Mt. Hight, 4,690 feet, and Zota Pass. Back up to the Carter Ridge and over South Carter, Little Carter, and North Carter, all affording excellent panoramic views of the Presidentials. On over the Moriah Ridge and down, very tired, to Gorham, New Hampshire.

Now with less than three hundred miles to go, I look forward to Maine and a grand finale of fall colors.

TEN

Out of Gorham, New Hampshire, and I leave the Whites be-hind and enter the golds and reds of autumn. Birches are tinged with a fringe of gold, and red maples blaze among the greens. I walk along through a hemlock forest—silent and still. The mist among the trees reflects the morning sun. On up to a beaver pond, and a great blue heron flies overhead. Silver rod, goldenrod, sharp-toothed asters, and panicled hawkweed surround the pond.

U p and up through hemlock, birch, and maple to Dream Lake. Autumn colors reflected and merged on the ripples of the lake and far across the mighty profile of the Presidentials. On into the Mohoosuc Mountains through spruce, filled with mushrooms and my first signs of moose. I sat on a road by a beaver pond called Moss Pond. A loon swam, and a dove appeared, while a small red-tailed hawk swooped for the huge blue dragonflies. Far on the other side, a beaver moved among the weeds. Suddenly the wind sent a whirl through the trees; a squirrel chattered, frogs croaked, and I moved on to Gentian Pond up some steep climbs to the ridge. The autumn aroma of dry leaves filled the air. On up the long, steep climb of Mt. Success and a view of southern Maine.

Finally, after thirteen states and over four months, I cross the border into Maine. I've come a long way, but the trip is far from over. Ahead still lie three hundred of the roughest miles of the trail.

On up over Carle Mountain and past Carol shelter. On up Goose Eye Mountain. I sat on the rocky summit looking back over the Whites and Presidentials until the clouds covered the sun. I moved on over North Peak, and then steeply down and across a plateau to Full Goose shelter, which was full. I sat on my tarp in the spruce, meditated, ate, and went to bed early.

Tomorrow I have the notorious Mohoosuc Notch to deal with.

Up early and I began the steep descent into the notch—a sharp boulder-filled gap between Goose Eye and Mohoosuc Mountains. The U.S. Marines couldn't have built a better obstacle course. The trail went over, under, around, and through the boulders. Several times I had to take my pack off and drag it through narrow crevasses between and under rocks. Patches of ice remained in this rock refrigerator. Finally, out of the rubble to a small stream. A hummingbird buzzed around the goldenrod and asters. At least the notch was flat. Now up steeply on a rocky, rooty trail up Mohoosuc and Old Speck, 4,180 feet. The trail down Speck was a new relocation and was graded—a pleasant break. A mosaic of colored maple leaves covered the ground as I descended along a cascading brook into Grafton Notch. I arrived at Grafton Notch shelter just as the rain began. I meditated and sat on my sleeping bag watching the rain and resting my weary bones.

It rained all night. I awoke to a cloudy morning. The brooks swelled, and the waterfall near the lean-to was full. I broke my bootlace this morning. Just as I left the lean-to, a mink ran in front of me. The weather gradually worsened and grew colder as I climbed Baldpate Mountain. As I neared the open summit, I donned my long pants, sweatshirts, rain chaps, and poncho. The frigid wind-driven rain stung as I climbed the bare rocks. I moved quickly across the open summit to get to the shelter of the tree line. I fell several times on the slick rocks as I descended. On along beautiful Frye Brook with its canyons, cascades, and waterfalls. I cooked a hot lunch at Frye Brook lean-to, warmed up, and dried out. Moved on down the wet overgrown trail, my boots saturated, to Squirrel Rock lean-to. I started a roaring fire, huddled close, and dried out my clothes.

Woke up to the pleasant sight of a sunny morning and ate a hot break-fast and moved on through the lichen-speckled spruce. On up Elephant Mountain with a babbling, sparkling brook on one side and a bank of birch and spruce on the other. Peeling paper birch shed its skin, unraveling itself in scrolls telling its history. A chirping red squirrel darted about the forest floor green with wood sorrel. Some helpful hiker left a note in a plastic bag warning of a beehive ahead. Again the forest burst forth with autumn colors in mirror images of springtime when it burst forth with new life. All summer

Mahoosuc Notch, Maine.

it gathered the colors of the sun to nourish that life. Now the forest gives it all back in gratitude and leaves its offerings to the wind.

Slept under a spruce by a stream. Woke to a chattering squirrel, meditated, and moved on to Sabbath Day Pond—a beautiful clear lake, sun shining on the wind-driven whitecaps. The candles of magenta fireweed burst into feathery flames, the lacy smoke carrying the seeds on the wind. On into Rangely, Maine, to pick up a care package from the post office. It turned out to be Labor Day—a day off in the real world, so I had to wait. Stayed at Viola's Guest House. I put up her storm windows, and she put me up and fed me.

I got my package and left town as the rain began. On up Saddleback Mountain in the rain—another cold dash for the tree line. On to Popular Ridge lean-to to wait out the storm. This was the first lean-to with a pole floor—not too comfortable, but it was dry. The greens of the trees faded off into the fog. The rain beat on the roof, and I snuggled into my sleeping bag. It rained all night, and I awoke to a foggy morning.

The clouds broke as I ascended Mt. Sugar Loaf, 4,237 feet, but again the summit was socked in. It began to rain as I descended through the ski area, and I sweated and struggled up the Bigelows to Horn Pond lean-to. I got right into my sleeping bag and cooked some hot soup and fratina to warm up.

I awoke to another miserable, cold, foggy morning. I moved on across Avery Peak, 4,180 feet, and Little Bigelow and a rough, rocky trail made worse by the frigid fog. On down past the shores of Flagstaff Lake, and now the rain stopped and so did I. I was exhausted. I set up my tarp by a spring, meditated, and went to sleep, hoping for a sunny morning.

It was a gray dawn, but the sun broke through. On past Carry Pond, with whitecaps. Shells of beechnuts were scattered on the trail. Bracken ferns drooped from the rain. A pileated woodpecker broke the silence. On through a pine forest. I met George and Rory again at Pierce Pond. The sun set into the purple haze over the lake, and the laughter of the loons echoed in the distance. We started a fire and watched the stars grow and glow.

George, Dan, and Rory, the trekking dog.

I woke to the call of loons and meditated on the rocks by the pond as the rising sun shone silver on the water. Today we left quickly to get to the Kennebec River early. The river is used to run logs to paper mills, and at about 10 A.M. they open the dam to flood the river. Crossing must be made before this. We got there in plenty of time, donned sneakers, and carefully waded across the river. The rocks were slippery and the current strong, but the water was only up to my knees. On into the little town of Caratunk with its old houses and streets lined with colorful sugar maples. Stopped at the general store, post office, and gas station—all in one. Had a snack and moved on past Pleasant Pond. On over Pleasant Mountain and down to Moxie Pond. On through green "beech light" into Joe's Hole Brook lean-to.

Out to another rainy day, and Moxie Bald with no views, and into Monson, Maine, stopping at Ken's Place—an old church converted into a hiker's haven, with George, Dan, and others.

Southern Maine has been rather disappointing because of the weather. All the major mountain views have been obscured. But you can't stop the rain, and I'm looking forward to the grand finale—the last 120 miles to the mountain of the morning sun—Mt. Katahdin.

ELEVEN

As the golden leaves drift to the ground, I drift along on the breeze out of Monson, Maine. On along fern-lined country roads and into the woods on muddy logging roads. The buzz of a chain saw in noisy battle against the balance of nature. With a crash, a living work of nature's wonder is reduced to mere wood or paper. The lofty pines—their roots knead the body of life in the earth; their voice speaks the message of the wind; their arms gather all the rays of the sun. The tree—our connection between heaven and earth. From a tree, to a log, to a board. From a thing of beauty to a thing of use. The greatest use I find for a tree is to sit in its shade, close my eyes, and let my free spirit fly. You don't have to cut down the trees to see the sun.

S oft gray columns of young beech trees, leaves flickering yellow sunlight as the path narrows into the woods. Out into a meadow. The ripples of grasses are ripe with seed in an array of autumn amber. Here
and there were yellow patches of flaming ferns. On down to Little Wilson's
Stream with stone remnants of the site of Savage's Mills. On along the stream
past cascading Little Wilson Falls and out onto more logging roads. Down
the road, through Bodfish Interval, along Long Pond Stream to Long Pond
Stream lean-to. Here again I met Dan, George and Rory, Trailboss Jack, and
Hammurabi (Bob) of the Cinci Boys. The lean-to sat in a spruce forest on a
bank overlooking the stream. A good peaceful spot with some good friends.

Got up early the next morning and meditated as the sun awakened the
forest greenery. Had a quick breakfast, splashed some icy stream water on
my face, and moved on toward Barren Mountain. On across a springy peat
bog with amber ferns and patches of pitcher plants. Great glowing green
masses of moss mattresses shone in the sunlight. Up steeply to the open
rocky summit of Barren Mountain. Looking carefully at the pond below, I
saw moose wading on the water's edge. Across the valley, Gulf Hagus, West
and Hay Mountains were visible. The pointed peaks of Saddleback Junior lay to
the east. On over Fourth and Third Mountains to Chairback Gap lean-to, where
I met a group from the Colby College Outing Club who maintain this section
of the trail. Dan and George caught up. The afternoon grew cloudy, windy, and
very cold. We all sat around a warm fire and became warm friends.

I got up in the dark of the night and was met by a sky full of stars. An
unexpected surprise. I arose into a sunny, cold, crisp morning and walked
on the new soft, mellow trail. With George I forded the Pleasant River and
moved on through pleasant sunlight forests. Moose sign was everywhere,
but they stayed well hidden. On over Gulf Hagus Mountain, 2,683 feet. I
stopped for a break. George went on, and Dan caught up with me. Together

Dan and I climbed in the warm sun up West Peak. As we reached the summit, we froze in our tracks, struck by the same force at the same time.

There, off in the not too distant north, is our first glimpse of our last mountain. After 1,900 miles, now looming so near, stands the Mountain of the Morning Sun—the mountain that glows in the first rays of the rising sun—the mountain that will know the last steps of this journey, the proverbial pot of gold—Mt. Katahdin.

Mt. Katahdin.

After a long, motionless silence, reflecting as the sun reflects off the open summit of Katahdin, I let out a yell that echoed off the mountains and rang through the valleys and maybe even shook the rocks of Mt. Katahdin. Dan and I were now whooping and dancing—our uproar answered and added to by George who was sitting awestruck right around a bend. After our brief celebration, we moved on, keeping an almost constant view of Katahdin, or "Ktaadn," as Thoreau spelled it in his journal on the Maine woods. Ktaadn is a Penobscot Indian word meaning "highest land." Quite appropriate for the way I was feeling.

On over Hay Mountain. The summit was an obstacle course of blow-downs. Trees were down everywhere, the trail lost in the tangle. After some maneuvering we made our way around and down the steep trail to familiar White Cap Mountain lean-to. I stayed here last year during my hike from Mt. Katahdin to Monson. In effect, I completed the entire Appalachian Trail in Monson, as I had done this section before. Dan was met by a friend who had some fresh vegetables—we all ate well.

Up and out early in the cold, clear air. Very mellow walking along old woods roads. These roads were overgrown but still smooth enough to be able to forget my feet and let my mind wander through the woods. On along East Branch River to East Branch Road lean-to for lunch. I didn't get far before I ran out of trail—the blazes went right through a beaver pond— or the beaver pond went right over the trail—whichever, I still had to find a dry route around. I made a circular route over the beaver dam and fought my way through the brush and back to the trail—but not for long. Again I went bog hopping. On through beech, yellow, black, and gray birch with smatterings of hemlocks and pines.

George, not a hundred yards ahead of me, spotted a young black bear on his hind legs against a tree. The bear was long gone before I got a look. On to Cooper Brook Falls lean-to. I stayed here last year also.

I took a bath in the frigid pool below the falls and dried in the sun. I decided to move on for a night alone. Found a good spot in a white pine forest on a hill overlooking a small pond and marsh. A good place to see moose and bear. I set up my tarp on the pine needles, meditated, and then made a tea of pine needles. Pine needle tea is rich in vitamin C and was very soothing. I hung my food and pack out of bear reach, then sat on a rock by my pond. A kingfisher shot by a few times, but no moose appeared. During the night I heard what I believed was a bear foraging near my camp.

The wind picked up and tried its best to lift my tarp from the soft pine needle ground. I got up early and got ready to move out just as the rain started. On through the "drisk," as Thoreau termed Maine's drizzle mist. Past a mud pond and along the shore of Lower Joe Mary Lake, on past Old Antlers Camp with a few old cabins. Met up with Hammurabi of the Cinci boys and walked on to Potaywadjo Spring lean-to. His brother Zoogie caught up, and we took a break and watched the rain. I went on ahead past Pemadumcook Lake, on through a marsh area, trying my best to find a dry route through. Finally out to a logging road; the rain was now heavy. On down the wet road to Nahwakanta Lake lean-to. The gray lake and the gray sky were one—connected by the rain between.

At the lean-to were Trailboss Jack and Napper of the Cinci boys, George and Rory, and soon Zoogie and Hammurabi caught up. Had a quick snack and moved on with Jack. It was too cold and wet to sit around. On through the dark, wet woods. Up ahead in the murky drisk, three large silhouettes moved slowly near the trail. I motioned for Jack to stop and got out my camera. We moved ahead slowly, and out of the mist appeared a moose family. A proud papa moose with a medium-size velvet rack, a mama moose, and a baby moose. They stood 25 feet off the trail, watching us with mild interest as they munched. We watched from this distance for a while, then decided it was best not to linger too close for too long.

We moved on through the foggy fir forest and through more of Maine's marshy menagerie. The wet woods were lush with moss and rot. On past Wadleigh Pond lean-to, and we were treated to another surprise. This one took the furry form of a black bear cub drinking from a small stream. We watched him bounce and bound off into the bushes. We moved on cautiously, looking for mama bear, but she didn't appear.

On through the rain to Rainbow Stream lean-to, another familiar place from the past. The shelter is in a hollow in the spruce forest with the stream in front. I jumped in and scraped some of Maine's mud off my legs. Jack did the same, along with the rest of the guys now arriving. Spent a crowded but high and dry night, got up and out before dawn to get ahead in hopes of seeing more wildlife. I spotted a cow moose grazing in a pond, with her head almost entirely submerged— a beautiful Maine wilderness scene set against the background of changing leaves.

On along Rainbow Lake with windblown, sun-sparkling whitecaps. On up to Rainbow Ledges—a broad rock tableland sparsely covered with golden beech trees. I sat in the sun, looking back. Over to the side loomed Katahdin. It sat like a huge birthday cake decorated with flaming fall colors.

On down through the "beech light," past Hurd Brook lean-to, and down to Abol Bridge, over the Penobscot River. Katahdin hung like a glowing cloud over the earth. I climbed Katahdin via the Appalachian Trail last year, so this year I went from Abol Bridge around the mountain to Roaring Brook to climb the north side through the Great Basin.

Moose at Chimney Pond, Maine, with Mt. Katahdin looming behind.

From the road and store at Abol Bridge, the trail follows the Penobscot River, then branches off along Nesowadnehunk Stream into Baxter State Park. It goes on past Big and Little Niagara Falls with deep pools and outstanding views of

Katahdin. On past Daicey Pond to Katahdin Stream camp-ground. From here the climb of Katahdin begins. Up through the fir and spruce past the cascading Katahdin Falls. Above the tree line Maine unfolds below. Lakes and hills and trees as far as you can see. The wind chants through the pines as you climb this mountain temple. The mountain turns into a huge loose pile of rocks that seem to have fallen like rain from heaven. Up you scramble, thinking that the summit is in sight, only to round the first crest and see miles more mountain rising to the sky. In some places handholds are driven into the rocks to aid in the difficult climb. Suddenly you find yourself standing on broad, flat tableland covered with lichens. On in the sun toward the top of Maine. Past Thoreau Spring and up over a narrow spine of boulders to Baxter Peak, the northern terminus of the Appalachian Trail.

I got to Roaring Brook campsite on a beautiful clear evening and prepared to climb the next morning. I sat and watched the gold-tinged evening clouds drift past this long-awaited mountain. I sat in a trance as the golds of the evening faded into the blues and grays of night. The stars appeared, and Katahdin in the moonlight glow was silhouetted against the night sky.

I awoke to a cloudy rainy morning. All the trails were closed, as it had snowed on the summit during the night. My wish was answered—I wanted at least one snowstorm while on the trail—a taste of all four seasons. Now, on my last day—my last mountain—the snow fell.

🌲🌲

In the last five months, I've lived close to the earth, close to spirit. I've seen how all life is provided for, how life flows through everything. I've become a part of it all, and all things have flowed to me—my dreams, my wishes answered, my heart and my soul opened.

🌲🌲

Spent the day relaxing and reflecting. Up before dawn the next day, I meditated and watched the morning star melt into the blue of the new day. I left my pack at the ranger station and walked under the cloudless sky toward Chimney Pond at the base of the mountain. Again I had the opportunity of meeting another moose family. The bull and calf were on one side of the trail, the cow on the other, and I was in the middle. This isn't the best position to be in, so I didn't linger too long. After another half mile, I rounded a corner and stood face to face with a young bull moose. He was alone, and we became good friends. I took his picture from three feet before he went back in the woods. On up on Chimney Pond, a small pond and campsite right in the bottom of the Great Basin. Cliffs over four thousand feet high formed a horseshoe around me. The jagged cliffs of the Knife Edge Trail cut the sky to the left, Hamlin Ridge to the right and straight ahead. Poking a hole in the sky was Baxter Peak—5,267 feet.

Knife Edge Trail, Mt. Katahdin, Maine.

I stand in the midst of this great cathedral. I raise my hands and offer myself to it. I bow my head and humble myself before this great temple of nature. I let myself be engulfed by it as I begin climbing the Cathedral Trail. Straight up the lichen-covered boulders. I feel the sun on my back and the cold of the rock on my hands. I cleanse myself by eating the pure, fresh first snow offered to me on the young pine branches. Up to the top—I stand alone in the wind, in the sun. The full force of the earth flows through me as I raise my arms to the sky. The Appalachian Trail stretches out before me. Tears flow from the depths of my soul, fall to the rocks, and trickle back two thousand miles. Tears of love to flow with the river of life and nourish all that is free. Tears that have seen the flow of the seasons add another ring to the tree of life.

The Cinci boys and George come up via the Appalachian Trail. We share champagne and memories, shake hands, and go off in our own directions knowing that friends thus made will again cross on the path of life. A moment at once joyous and sad. The joy of seeing dreams come true. The sadness of knowing that all things must pass. But tears and laughter arise from the same source, and all my journeys are but stepping-stones to my universal dream.

I hang up my boots at the end of the Appalachian Trail.

ACKNOWLEDGMENTS

Although I hiked the Appalachian Trail alone, every step was strengthened by the support I received from so many. First and foremost was my mother, Lillian, Lill the Flower Lady, who made the love of nature a natural part of my life. She also instilled in me self-reliance and the assurance that any path was possible if I was willing to take the first step.

The screen door would slam on a Saturday morning, and Marge and Mike Jason would stride through our back porch in Cheshire, Connecticut, and pore over A.T. maps with me. By the third cup of coffee, we'd be halfway to Maine. Dr. Louise Armbruster, our family doctor throughout my childhood in Cheshire and a woods woman herself, encouraged me to keep walking and to keep writing.

I have special gratitude for my friends at the *Cheshire Herald*, then a very hometown newspaper, for publishing the periodic entries that form the backbone of this book. At that time, I considered Cheshire my hometown, and I was proud to bring images of my wandering world back to the hearth. Not only did the *Cheshire Herald* print the account of my 1975 A.T. hike, it also featured stories from my five years as a Peace Corps Volunteer in the Central African Republic. This was a forum for me to reflect on experiences very different from those in small town Connecticut, foreign, yet familiar in the challenges we all faced.

I walked this trail in 1975, and I'm finally getting back to these words in 2014, after almost 40 years. The stories have been woven through family and friends, and the Appalachian Trail became part of the life of my children Deva and Orion. My wife, Doreen, encouraged me to reach my dream, and my four-year-old, son Dylan, may learn more about his dad through these words. My dear sister, Lynn, transcribed and translated my handwritten, trail-smudged, chicken-scratch notes to my friends at the *Herald*. Nancy Kittle, a kind and keen supporter of the World Wildlife Fund's Africa Program, which I led for the past 30-some odd years, believed in the story and helped put it into a Word document. Jennifer Koontz, an old friend and a New Yorker copy editor, has worked wonders bringing some sense of order to my musings. Kathleen Payne added needed structure and made substantial editorial contributions. I want to thank Marian Beil and John Coyne at Peace Corps Writers for their great help in this work.

To John Collins, the Cinci Boys, and all the friends I walked a mile with or shared a shelter with along the way, I cherish the memories of those short five months in 1975, and am glad to have this journal to keep the memories alive.

And finally, to every flower I contemplated, every mountaintop I caressed, every stream I soaked sore feet in, I owe my life. I hope that my life's work in conservation has helped to keep life alive in the Appalachians, in Africa, in Cheshire, to honor the legacy of Lill the Flower Lady.

www.ingramcontent.com/pod-product-compliance
Lightning Source LLC
Chambersburg PA
CBHW060810050426
42449CB00008B/1611